Living Free and Green

A Practical Guide to Off-Grid Independence

Morgan Lawson

Table of Contents

INTRODUCTION

The rush of contemporary life is making people yearn for a more straightforward, environmentally friendly style of existence that embraces self-sufficiency and cultivates a closer relationship with the natural world. "Living Free and Green: A Practical Guide to Off-Grid Independence" offers a thorough introduction to off-grid living to empower those who want to abandon the limitations of traditional living and adopt a sustainable and independent way of life.

This book provides a roadmap for people who want to live off the grid and create their path to a more independent life, not merely a set of theoretical ideas. We will delve into the nuances of off-grid living, highlighting its benefits and drawbacks and assisting you in deciding if this way of life is appropriate for you. Every chapter offers helpful advice and doable actions, covering everything from building eco-friendly houses and growing your food to choosing the best off-grid site and utilizing renewable energy sources.

You'll learn the trade secrets of ecologically friendly building, water independence, and sustainable energy as we turn the pages. We'll explore how to cultivate your food, properly manage waste, and use off-grid technology to improve your day-to-day living. Financial independence will be examined in an off-grid environment, along with methods for resolving typical problems and creating a welcoming community.

"Living Free and Green" is an essential resource whether your ideal off-grid community is a cooperative off-grid community, a remote lodge in the woods, or any combination. This e-book, jam-packed with practical guidance, suggestions, and abundant resources, is your journey companion as you embrace a life of liberty, sustainability, and off-grid independence.

CHAPTER I

Understanding Off-Grid Living

Advantages and Benefits

The decision to adopt a lifestyle independent of the grid represents a significant step toward self-sufficiency and sustainability. This lifestyle, which was once considered an alternative, is gaining popularity as individuals seek to escape the trappings of metropolitan life and decrease their impact on the environment. Living off the grid has several advantages and benefits beyond independence alone. These advantages and benefits involve a holistic approach to living harmoniously with nature, preserving resources, and cultivating a more aware existence.

One of the most significant benefits of living off the grid is its increased independence level. Off-grinders are individuals not independent of the conventional grid to meet their energy requirements. Instead, they rely on renewable power sources such as solar, wind, and hydropower. Because of this autonomy, individuals are less reliant on fossil fuels and are protected from the oscillations in the prices of utilities and the power outages that can occur. A compelling motivation for many people to embark on the road of off-grid living is the ability to create their power sustainably, which is especially important in light of climate change and other environmental concerns.

In addition, living off the grid helps you cultivate a profound connection with the universe around you. Individuals can appreciate the changing of the seasons, the rhythm of the Earth, and the one-of-a-kind beauty of their surroundings when they choose to spend their time in a region surrounded by nature. This relationship with nature is not only appealing to the eye, but it also contributes to the individual's mental well-being. Research has demonstrated that being near natural landscapes and green spaces can aid in reducing stress, improving cognitive function, and enhancing overall pleasure. Off-grid living, which focuses on selecting settings resonant with natural beauty, makes it possible to live a lifestyle that encourages a more fundamental connection with the Earth.

One more significant advantage of living off the grid is achieving financial independence. Even though the early setup expenditures could appear intimidating, the long-term savings are substantial. Following establishing a sustainable infrastructure, the ongoing costs associated with utilities are reduced to a reasonable level. For example, solar panels and wind turbines provide free and abundant energy, and rainwater collection systems lessen reliance on municipal water sources. Other examples include biomass energy and solar energy. Off-grinders frequently discover that they can significantly reduce their monthly expenses over time, which provides them the freedom to make decisions regarding their finances and the flexibility to transfer resources to other elements of their lives.

A further advantage of living off the grid is that it enables individuals to exercise control over their food source by utilizing organic and sustainable methods. Those who live off the grid can ensure that they have access to fresh and healthful food by establishing gardens, embracing permaculture principles, and keeping livestock. Not only does this lessen the dependency on commercial agriculture, but it also offers a more in-depth comprehension of the origins of food and the methods used to create it. The advantages extend to one's physical health, as the produce grown at home is typically more nutrient-dense, and cultivating one's own food is inherently physically demanding and physically fulfilling.

Living off the grid has several advantages, the most convincing of which are the environmental advantages. In the traditional sense, homes connected to the grid are frequently associated with excessive energy usage, which contributes to pollution and emissions of greenhouse gases. On the other hand, off-grid living emphasizes sustainability by utilizing renewable energy sources, careful water management, and environmentally friendly building materials. Conscious decisions made by individuals dedicated to living in harmony with the environment are directly responsible for decreasing the carbon footprint.

Living off the grid also helps cultivate a sense of resiliency and readiness. Those who choose this way of life frequently acquire various abilities, ranging from fundamental survival strategies to behaviors that promote sustainable living. The capacity to generate power, harvest water, and cultivate food autonomously becomes a precious asset, particularly in times of crisis or catastrophe. With a self-sufficiency that is both empowering and practical, off-grinders are equipped to weather issues such as power outages, water shortages, or disruptions in the food supply chain. Off-grinders can weather these challenges on their own.

Additionally, a significant benefit is the sense of community that frequently emerges in environments that are not connected to the grid. Off-gridders often create deep ties with one another based on shared beliefs and common aims, regardless of whether they live alone or within a community of folks who share similar values and interests. The members of these communities assist one another by exchanging labor, resources, and information. This sense of camaraderie contributes to an overall improvement in the off-grid experience by reducing the potential difficulties associated with being isolated and building an environment that encourages collaboration.

It is important to note that the advantages and benefits of living off the grid go well beyond disconnecting from the conventional grid. A holistic approach to sustainable living is incorporated into this lifestyle choice, which encourages autonomy, a profound connection with nature, financial freedom, and environmental stewardship. Off-grid living is a practical and gratifying choice for people who aim to live a free, environmentally conscious life in tune with the Earth. This kind of living is becoming increasingly popular as people look for alternatives to traditional ways of living. The road toward off-grid independence is not merely a break from the usual; instead, it is a deliberate move toward a more balanced, intentional, and rewarding way of life.

Challenges and Considerations

Off-grid life, while appealing, comes with its own set of unique challenges and considerations. Embarking on this journey requires forethought, flexibility, and a determination to overcome obstacles. For those who aspire to live off the grid, understanding and managing the complexities of renewable energy sources and isolation's social and psychological impacts is crucial. Yet, overcoming these challenges brings a sense of accomplishment and fulfillment that is unparalleled in traditional living.

Choosing the right location for off-grid living is a significant challenge. Practical considerations must be balanced against the allure of a scenic, isolated environment. Access to essentials like water can make a huge difference. Evaluating water availability for consumption, irrigation, and power generation is crucial, even if being close to nature is a priority. Understanding local climate, zoning laws, and property restrictions are also important. Thorough research and collaboration with local authorities are necessary to ensure the chosen location meets the practical demands of sustainable living and legal standards. Making these informed decisions empowers individuals to create a sustainable, legally compliant, off-grid lifestyle.

Off-grid life is based on the goal of energy independence, which presents several difficulties. Planning and funding are necessary for using renewable energy sources like solar, wind, or hydropower. Due to the high upfront expenses of installing solar panels, wind turbines, and energy storage devices, people must carefully plan and budget for their off-grid energy needs. In addition, the variable nature of renewable energy sources makes it difficult to maintain a steady electricity supply, particularly in regions vulnerable to bad weather. Backup generators and adaptable energy storage technologies become crucial elements to mitigate these issues and maintain a consistent and dependable power supply in the face of variations.

Another essential factor to consider when living off the grid is water management. The practicality of living off the land might be complicated, even though the idealized version may entail depending only on natural water supplies. Although they are a popular option, the effectiveness of rainwater harvesting systems depends on local precipitation patterns. Wells and groundwater supplies need to be carefully managed to prevent depletion. Water filtration and purification systems are also required to guarantee a clean and safe water supply. Off-grinders confront a complex problem in balancing long-term sustainability with daily demands, agricultural requirements, and energy generation while conserving water.

Off-grid construction has particular difficulties with sustainable building materials and environmentally friendly architecture. Although reducing the environmental impact is of the utmost importance, the cost and availability of these materials may need to be improved. A sophisticated strategy is required to strike a balance between a building that considers the environment and practical factors. Off-grinders frequently discover they must investigate alternate construction techniques like cob, straw bale, or salvaged materials. This creates a learning curve as people adjust to non-traditional building techniques and ensure their constructions satisfy off-grid living and legal requirements.

Living off the grid might present psychological challenges due to social and physical isolation. The attraction of peace can quickly give way to a feeling of isolation, particularly for people used to the social dynamics of city life. Feelings of disconnection and loneliness may result from living far away from services, neighbors, and community centers. A sensation of isolation may also result from the absence of customary social amenities, including dining establishments, entertainment centers, and planned activities. Intentional attempts to create a social support network are necessary to overcome this obstacle, whether they involve nearby off-grid communities or use contemporary communication tools to stay in touch with the outside world.

Emergency preparedness is an essential factor to consider when living off the grid. Living off the land requires one to be highly mindful of potential hazards, which can include everything from natural disasters to power outages and water shortages. Off-grinders must have the knowledge and tools to deal with crises head-on. This includes having emergency food and water supplies, backup power sources, and a working knowledge of basic survival and first aid procedures. Successful off-grid life is characterized by flexibility in the face of unforeseen obstacles, and being ready becomes essential to maintaining a secure environment.

Transitioning to off-grid living presents financial challenges. While the potential for financial independence and long-term savings on utility bills are significant benefits, initial setup costs can be substantial. Purchasing and installing renewable energy systems, constructing eco-friendly buildings, and implementing sustainable water and waste management techniques require a significant upfront investment. Careful financial planning and discipline are necessary when budgeting for these costs and planning for ongoing maintenance and improvements. Despite these challenges, off- grinders often find that the long-term benefits far outweigh the initial costs, instilling a sense of resilience and determination in their financial planning.

Off-grid waste handling poses particular difficulties. The unavailability of traditional waste disposal services often calls for other approaches. For organic waste, composting becomes essential, and recycling becomes even more crucial to reduce environmental effects. Off-grinders must embrace minimizing trash generation by reusing, repurposing, and decreasing. It takes constant work and creativity to create closed-loop systems where waste products support the sustainability of the living environment.

Although choosing to live off the grid has its share of difficulties and considerations, it also has unmatched benefits for people dedicated to sustainability and independence. The off-grid lifestyle necessitates a thorough and deliberate strategy, encompassing everything from choosing the right site and utilizing renewable energy sources to managing water supplies, building environmentally responsible structures, and attending to the psychological effects of isolation.

Practical knowledge, flexibility, and a solid commitment to adopting a sustainable and self-sufficient lifestyle are necessary to overcome these obstacles. By taking on these challenges head-on, people can realize the full benefits of off-grid living and lead satisfying lives adaptable to change and environmentally responsible.

Is Off-Grid Living Right for You?

The allure of off-grid living, with its promise of independence, sustainability, and a deeper connection with nature, captivates many who seek a different lifestyle. However, embarking on this path to self- sufficiency requires careful consideration to ensure it aligns with one's situation. This involves introspection of personal values and lifestyle preferences and a realistic assessment of the challenges and responsibilities that come with off-grid living.

One's values and priorities play a pivotal role in determining the suitability of off-grid living. Those attracted to this lifestyle often share a commitment to environmental sustainability, a yearning for greater independence, and a desire for a simpler life. Evaluating how these ideals align with the realities of off-grid living is essential. Are you ready to trade city comforts for a lifestyle that requires manual labor to meet basic needs? Off-grid living typically demands a simpler, more intentional lifestyle and a solid environmental responsibility.

The suitability for off-grid living hinges on a frank assessment of resourcefulness and adaptability. Off-grinders must be prepared to tackle challenges such as sourcing alternative energy, managing water resources effectively, and building sustainable structures. Learning new skills, adapting to changing circumstances, and solving technical issues are crucial. Off-grid living requires a level of self-sufficiency that may be unfamiliar to those accustomed to modern conveniences. Therefore, those contemplating this lifestyle change must be ready to invest time and effort in acquiring the necessary skills and knowledge for successful off-grid living.

An important factor in determining whether off-grid living is feasible is location. The practicalities of choosing a suitable location cannot be emphasized, despite the romantic vision of a secluded cabin in the woods being alluring. Important considerations include being close to necessary resources, having access to renewable energy sources, and following local laws. An off-grid area that combines functionality and natural beauty is excellent. To ensure that the chosen place fits their goal of independent and sustainable living, people must carefully investigate possible areas before committing to this lifestyle. They should consider factors like water availability, climate, and legal implications.

An essential factor in assessing whether off-grid life is appropriate is considering family or individual dynamics. While some people thrive on isolation, others could find off-grid isolation complicated. Evaluating social contact, education, and healthcare needs for individuals and families is crucial. The success and happiness of living off the grid also stem from the capacity to work together with family members in embracing a shared off-grid lifestyle vision. The success of the off-grid lifestyle within the family largely depends on open communication and a shared commitment to it.

Being financially stable is vital for anyone thinking about living off the grid. The possibility of financial independence and long-term utility bill savings are alluring, but there might be significant setup expenditures upfront. It costs a lot of money upfront to buy and install renewable energy systems, build environmentally friendly buildings, and use sustainable water and waste management techniques. People need to budget for these costs carefully, considering possible improvements and ongoing maintenance. Being financially prepared keeps people from becoming overwhelmed by unforeseen expenses and guarantees that the transition to off-grid living is a feasible and sustainable task.

Before deciding to live off the grid, people should consider how feasible it would be to meet their basic needs independently. Planning and execution are crucial for producing food, energy, and water. Off-grinders must be willing to put in the time and effort necessary to set up and maintain these vital systems. Solar panels and wind turbines are sustainable energy sources that require careful installation and upkeep. Management and rainwater harvesting systems must be maintained to guarantee a steady water supply. It takes dedication to everyday tasks and a commitment to mastering agricultural skills to cultivate gardens and potentially raise cattle. Living off the grid means you have to be willing to take an active role in protecting these essential elements of day-to-day living.

Those thinking of living off the grid should also be aware of this way of life's legal and regulatory ramifications. Respecting the many zoning laws, building codes, and environmental requirements is essential to living an off-grid, lawful, and sustainable life. Obtaining the required licenses for water access, alternative energy systems, and construction structures is crucial. Ignoring or getting around legal restrictions can cause problems and difficulties later on. Consequently, determining if off-grid living is correct requires carefully analyzing local laws and a dedication to following them.

Prospective off-grinders should also think about the psychological implications of this way of life. It can be mentally taxing to be alone, lack conventional social amenities, and be flexible. People who are used to the social dynamics of city living could find the change difficult. Off-grid living, however, may be advantageous for people who value peace of mind, solitude, and a closer relationship with the natural world. An honest assessment of one's preferences and a desire to accept the possible difficulties of leading a more reclusive lifestyle are necessary to determine one's psychological readiness.

In conclusion, deciding if off-grid life is the correct choice for you is a complex and multidimensional process. It necessitates thoughtful consideration of one's ideals, flexibility, financial readiness, and a profound comprehension of the realities of independent and sustainable living. Living off the grid is a lifestyle option that requires serious thought and dedication rather than a one-size-fits-all approach. A life of increased self-sufficiency, environmental stewardship, and a close bond with nature await those prepared to take on the difficulties and adapt their ideals to the requirements of off-grid living. These benefits can be life-changing.

CHAPTER II

Choosing the Right Location

Factors to Consider in Selecting Off-Grid Land

Choosing the appropriate piece of land is essential to a practical off-grid lifestyle. Whether or not to select a self-sufficient and sustainable lifestyle depends on several considerations beyond the visual appeal of a beautiful setting. Selecting off-grid land requires careful consideration of several elements, including the availability of necessary resources, legal issues, and environmental concerns.

Access to essential resources—water being the most important—is one of the first factors considered when choosing an off-grid territory. Water is necessary for agriculture, energy production, and human survival. Hence, its availability must be guaranteed. Prospective off-grinders should evaluate the local water supply before acquiring a plot of land. They should consider elements like good depth, water quality, and the water source's year-round sustainability. Rainwater harvesting is a widespread off-grid practice, but whether it fits with the region's water needs depends on its precipitation patterns. First and foremost, creating a sustainable off- grid existence requires reliable and ample access to water.

The area's climate is another important consideration, as it directly affects agricultural methods and energy production. Off-grinders must evaluate seasonal temperature variations, wind patterns, and sunlight levels to determine whether renewable energy sources like solar and wind turbines are viable. Planning for the installation and effectiveness of energy systems is aided by a thorough awareness of the local environment, which guarantees a consistent and dependable power supply. Furthermore, understanding the environment makes choosing suitable crops and gardening techniques easier, which adds to the off-grid lifestyle's overall self-sufficiency.

The terrain of the land significantly influences the practicality and attractiveness of living off the grid. The land's topography impacts the ease of access, drainage efficiency, and buildability. While low-lying places may be vulnerable to flooding, steep slopes may present difficulties when constructing buildings or cultivating land. An in-depth topographical survey gives off-grinders valuable information about possibilities and obstacles, enabling them to plan their land's growth and use. Additionally, the height of the land can affect weather patterns and temperature, which can affect gardening decisions and energy requirements.

When choosing off-grid land, accessibility to transportation and closeness to necessary facilities are essential but sometimes disregarded factors. While many off-gridders are drawn to the appeal of isolation, it's necessary to consider practical factors like accessibility to grocery stores, medical facilities, and other essentials. Determining the distance to the closest town or city aids in comprehending the advantages and possible drawbacks of solitude. Practical off-grid living also requires considering the state of access routes and how easy it is to travel throughout specific seasons.

Land selection must consider legal and regulatory factors to guarantee a seamless and legal off-grid living experience. Regional variations exist in zoning laws, construction rules, and environmental requirements, all of which need to be well-researched and comprehended. Off-gridders should find out what laws specifically apply to trash disposal, water use, and alternative energy systems in their selected area. Securing building permissions and following local laws are essential to steer clear of legal issues and guarantee a safe off-grid existence.

Many people who choose off-grid living do so because they believe that environmental stewardship is essential and land use should consider the surrounding ecology first. A comprehensive awareness of the environment is aided by evaluating the diversity of plant life, the ecological health of the land, and the existence of wildlife. Off-grinders ought to strive for a mutually beneficial coexistence with the environment, abstaining from actions that compromise nearby ecosystems and actively pursuing methods to augment biodiversity. The choice of land should align with conservation and preservation ideals, demonstrating a dedication to ethical and sustainable living.

When making decisions, economic considerations are also taken into account. Even if the initial cost of the property could be a significant factor, off-gridders also need to assess the location's long-term economic feasibility. Considerations should be made for things like property taxes, the possibility of earning income, and the general cost of life in the community. Knowing the state of the economy helps to guarantee that the off-grid property selection fits in with financial objectives and reality, promoting a prosperous and sustainable way of life.

Community dynamics can significantly impact the off-grid living experience, even though they are only sometimes a top concern for people looking for seclusion. Some people view a strong sense of community as essential to happy living because it fosters social interaction, cooperation, and the sharing of resources. Off-grinders interested in starting or joining a community should consider the existing dynamics, the availability of others who share their interests, and the possibility of mutual assistance. Enriching the overall experience of living off the grid, the community may be a source of strength and resilience when faced with difficulties.

Planning for future growth and development in the neighborhood is essential to protect against unanticipated events that can compromise the off-grid way of life. Even while there is no denying the allure of unspoiled wilderness, potential off-grinders need to investigate and prepare for any planned infrastructure developments or changes in the area. A comprehensive understanding of the potential for land use, urban development, and municipal legislation changes is necessary to make well-informed judgments regarding the off-grid lifestyle's long-term sustainability.

To sum up, choosing off-grid land is a complex process that involves a thorough comprehension of the property's features, legal issues, environmental impact, and individual objectives. The chosen land serves as a blank canvas on which the off-grid lifestyle is painted, affecting everything from electricity production to water availability to general self-sufficiency. Selecting land with consideration and knowledge guarantees that those who live off the grid are prepared to face the difficulties and enjoy a self-sufficient, rewarding, and sustainable off-grid lifestyle.

Climate and Environmental Considerations

The growing trend of off-grid living as a sustainable lifestyle option highlights the crucial interaction between environmental and climate concerns. Adopting a self-sufficient lifestyle and cutting off from the traditional grid are intrinsically linked to a dedication to environmental conservation. Navigating the convergence of climatic and environmental elements is vital for a successful and sustainable off-grid living experience, from choosing the ideal location with a climate favorable to renewable energy sources to reducing the ecological impact of off-grid behaviors.

One of the main pillars of off-grid life is climate considerations. The local climate directly impacts the efficiency and availability of renewable energy sources, such as wind turbines and solar panels. The quantity of sunlight and wind patterns strongly affects the viability and production of these systems. Off-grinders need to carefully evaluate the selected site's solar potential, considering variables like average daily sunshine, seasonal fluctuations, and shading from nearby buildings or natural features. Wind patterns should also be examined to evaluate whether wind energy systems are viable. Off-grinders can carefully build and install energy systems that maximize the potential of renewable resources by having a thorough awareness of the local climate.

Furthermore, one of the most critical factors in off-grid life is how the environment affects water availability. Off-grid residents' ability to maintain their independence depends on sustainable water management because the local climate directly impacts water sources. In off-grid communities, rainwater harvesting is a popular activity that depends on local precipitation patterns. Determining the viability of rainwater collection systems requires evaluating the average yearly rainfall and comprehending the seasonal changes. Off-grinders should also be aware of the possibility of droughts or water scarcity, as these circumstances can significantly influence the dependability of water sources. A sustained off-grid existence requires strategic water management plans incorporating conservation techniques and alternate sources.

In agriculture, the kinds of crops that can be cultivated successfully depend on the local climate. To augment food sources, off-grid living frequently entails planting personal gardens; therefore, it's critical to comprehend the growth season, temperature ranges, and frost dates. Crops suitable for the climate can flourish with minimal assistance, making them a more robust and sustainable food source. Moreover, the local climate influences pest and disease patterns, which helps off-grinders implement natural and environmentally beneficial gardening techniques. Off-grinders can establish a positive and fruitful relationship with the earth by coordinating their agricultural practices with the climate.

Climate considerations go beyond how off-grid systems and behaviors may be affected immediately; they also consider the larger picture of climate change. Because of how urgently global climate issues need to be addressed, off-grinders need to be more mindful of how climate change may affect their chosen places. Extreme weather events, changes in precipitation patterns, and rising temperatures can all affect how sustainable off-grid living is. A proactive strategy includes building off-grid structures to resist extreme weather and diversifying energy sources to reduce the risk of climate-induced changes in renewable resources. These are examples of climate resilience measures that can be incorporated into off-grid planning.

Achieving sustainable off-grid living requires taking climate elements and environmental concerns into account. Off-grinders have an innate desire to leave as little of an ecological imprint as possible, and all facets of their lifestyle, from waste management to energy production, should be planned with the environment in mind. One of the main strategies for reducing the environmental impact of off-grid living is eco-friendly design. Off-grid buildings have more minor ecological implications thanks to sustainable building materials, energy-efficient designs, and passive solar principles. These factors also improve the lifestyle's overall sustainability and efficiency.

An essential component of responsible off-grid living is water conservation. Off-grinders need to prioritize using natural and rainwater sources, reduce water consumption, and optimize the effectiveness of water storage and distribution systems. Off-grinders who care about the environment frequently install low-flow fixtures and water-efficient appliances and repurpose greywater for irrigation. Off-grinders help protect local ecosystems and water supplies by minimizing water consumption and improving water management.

One of the most critical environmental factors in off-grid living is waste management. Off-grinders take the maxim "reduce, reuse, recycle" to a whole new level as they work to reduce trash production and implement environmentally friendly waste disposal methods. An essential part of living off the grid is recycling, composting organic waste, and reusing objects for different uses. In addition to reducing waste's adverse effects on the environment, the idea is to develop closed-loop systems in which waste materials enhance the sustainability of the surrounding environment. An emphasis on ethical waste management reflects the off-grid lifestyle's larger environmental stewardship philosophy.

Off-grid living's environmental objectives are in line with the incorporation of renewable energy sources. Traditional grid-connected power sources can be replaced with clean, sustainable energy sources like solar panels, wind turbines, and other alternative energy systems. Off-grinders lessen dependency on fossil fuels and reduce the environmental impact of conventional energy generation by utilizing sun and wind power. Furthermore, off-grinders can now store excess energy for use when renewable resource availability is low, thanks to improvements in energy storage technologies, which help provide a more consistent and dependable off-grid energy supply.

Another environmental factor that off-gridders may actively support is biodiversity conservation. Choosing off-grid sites that sustain various ecosystems and taking action to save the local wildlife and plants both improve the state of the environment. Off-grinders can actively participate in environmental protection by planting native plants, protecting wildlife habitats, and abstaining from actions that degrade nearby ecosystems. Life in harmony with the natural world becomes a guiding concept, highlighting the connection between off-grid life and general environmental sustainability.

Regarding off-grid life, the value of environmental education cannot be emphasized. Off-gridders need to keep learning about their chosen area's unique ecosystems, climatic trends, and environmental difficulties. Decision-making processes are informed by this knowledge, guaranteeing that off-grid actions align with ecological sustainability. A sense of duty and stewardship is also fostered by environmental awareness, motivating off-grinders to actively contribute to the preservation and well-being of the surrounding natural environment.

In summary, the core of off-grid life is the intersection of environmental and climatic factors. Living a self-sufficient and sustainable lifestyle requires a thorough grasp of the local environment and how it affects agricultural operations, water availability, renewable energy sources, and other factors. Off-grinders are guided by environmental considerations when it comes to actively participating in responsible behaviors that improve the general health of the ecosystem, limiting their ecological imprint and supporting biodiversity. Off-grinders make a lifestyle that satisfies their needs while keeping the broader objectives of environmental sustainability and preservation by skillfully negotiating this complex confluence

Legal and Regulatory Aspects

Living off the grid is a radical step toward independence, self-sufficiency, and sustainability. But this path involves more than just picking the ideal spot and putting eco-friendly methods in place—it also involves comprehending and abiding by the legal and regulatory structures that control land use and alternative lifestyles. Off-grinders have to negotiate a complicated legal environment that differs significantly from one place to the next. This environment includes water rights, building requirements, zoning laws, and environmental regulations. This section delves into the legal and regulatory aspects of off-grid living, examining the obstacles and factors people must consider to guarantee a safe and legal off-grid lifestyle.

The cornerstones of the legal environment surrounding off-grid life are zoning rules and land-use regulations. Zoning regulations specify the uses of land and the kinds of buildings that are permitted in particular zones. Before choosing off-grid land, people need to learn about and comprehend the zoning laws that apply to the area they have in mind. While some areas may have unclear or antiquated zoning restrictions, others may have explicit legislation that allows or prohibits off-grid living. Off-gridders who are unsure are still determining rules that affect their plans should speak with the local planning offices. This procedure is necessary to prevent land use-related legal issues and obstacles.

Another critical factor for anyone starting an off-grid living is building codes. These rules provide construction standards and requirements that guarantee the buildings' structural integrity and safety. Off-grinders who want to design and build structures that adhere to safety and environmental regulations must be well-versed in the local construction rules. Existing building rules may need special notice of sustainable and environmentally friendly building methods, such as using alternative materials and renewable energy sources. By being aware of the legal constraints imposed by building codes, off-grinders can design ecologically responsible and legally compliant structures.

The legal framework for off-grid living is heavily influenced by environmental rules, especially in places with vulnerable ecosystems or conservation zones. Regulations controlling land management, garbage disposal, and water use must be known to off-gridders.

Septic tanks, water wells, and alternative energy systems occasionally need permissions or approvals. Respecting environmental laws is essential to reducing the adverse ecological effects of off-grid living and staying out of trouble with the law. Maintaining a harmonious cohabitation with the natural surroundings entails meeting local and regional environmental legislation and adhering to set criteria.

Water rights are crucial to the legal issues associated with off-grid living, particularly in areas where competing demands or water scarcity occur daily. A diverse legal framework governs water rights; some regions have clearly defined systems, while others rely on riparian rights or historical use. Off-grinders must be aware of the regulations controlling water rights in their selected area to guarantee that their access to water is both sustainable and lawful. Installing rainwater harvesting systems and digging wells necessitates adherence to local laws, and people should obtain the required licenses to prevent disputes over water use.

Recycling, greywater systems, composting toilets, and other alternative waste management techniques are standard in off-grid living. It is essential to comprehend trash disposal legislation to guarantee adherence to environmental and public health requirements. Particular waste disposal procedures or standards may apply in specific places when disposing of human waste. Off-grinders must comply with legal requirements while navigating these constraints to use ecologically responsible waste management procedures. People can lessen the possibility of garbage disposal-related legal issues and help preserve the environment by implementing sustainable waste management solutions.

One of the main components of off-grid living, renewable energy systems, can be subject to particular laws and approval procedures. Alternative energy sources like solar panels and wind turbines must abide by electrical rules and sometimes get local government permission. Off-grinders must ensure that their energy infrastructure complies with environmental and safety rules and become familiar with the legal requirements for establishing and maintaining renewable energy systems. Being informed of the law is essential to preventing fines, penalties, and outages related to off-grid power installations.

Off-grid life involves significant legal problems related to land ownership and tenure. While some off-gridders could decide to buy land altogether, others might consider other options, including long-term leases or shared ownership. Distinct ownership forms have different legal implications; thus, people must be aware of these. Legal contracts and agreements should be crafted appropriately to clearly describe rights, duties, and conflict resolution procedures, whether for the purchase of land or joint living. Off-gridders can live a more sustainable lifestyle with the assurance that their land ownership is based on a solid legal basis.

Managing legal and regulatory issues can be complicated in places with antiquated or restrictive rules that might not consider the unique characteristics of off-grid life. Residents living off the grid could face opposition or a lack of comprehension from local authorities because they need to familiarize themselves with alternative lifestyles. Education and advocacy are crucial in raising awareness and encouraging cooperation between regulatory agencies and off-grinders. Communicating honestly and openly with local authorities can help them better understand off-grid life and open the door to cooperative solutions that strike a balance between following the law and pursuing sustainable living.

When off-grinders have disagreements with neighbors, particularly in places where conventional and off-grid lives coexist, legal issues may come up. Disagreements that need to be resolved through the legal system may arise from differences in land use practices, noise levels, or aesthetics. Off-gridders must be ready to resolve disputes amicably and, if required, seek legal advice to safeguard their rights and interests. Ascertain Building trusting connections with neighbors and the community is essential to encouraging acceptance of the off-grid lifestyle and lowering the risk of legal issues.

To sum up, living off the grid's legal and regulatory elements are complex and multidimensional, necessitating a thorough knowledge of environmental rules, municipal laws, and codes. Living a sustainable lifestyle and cutting off from the traditional grid requires rigorous legal compliance. Off-grinders need to get involved with local government, carry out in-depth studies, and push for acceptance of alternative lifestyles. Through careful legal navigation and observance of current laws, people can create a stable basis for their off-grid living that satisfies legal requirements and the values of sustainability, independence, and self-sufficiency.

CHAPTER III

Sustainable Energy Sources

Solar Power Systems

Solar power shines in renewable energy, providing a steady source of electricity for individuals desiring independence from the grid. Off-grid living requires autonomy and self-sufficiency, making solar power systems essential. These solar energy solutions allow off-grinders to meet their electricity needs while reducing their environmental effect. This section examines solar power systems in off-grid living, including their components, benefits, obstacles, and how they transform a sustainable and independent existence.

Modern marvels like photovoltaic (PV) solar panels transform sunshine into electricity at the heart of solar power systems. Silicon-based semiconductors in these panels create electricity when exposed to sunlight. Each form of solar panel has its benefits and efficiency. Monocrystalline panels are efficient because they have one crystal structure. Multiple crystal configurations make polycrystalline panels cheaper. Thin-film solar panels, constructed of semiconductor layers, are lightweight and flexible, making them appropriate for many applications. Off-gridders can customize their solar panels based on money, space, and efficiency.

A complete solar power system captures, stores, and distributes electricity using solar panels and other components. Solar charge controllers avoid overcharging and optimize battery charging by regulating solar panel voltage and current. Off-grid solar arrays need batteries to store excess energy from sunny periods for usage during cloudy ones. Solar power systems use lead-acid, lithium-ion, and gel batteries, each with capacities, lifespans, and maintenance needs. Solar panels provide direct current (DC), which inverters convert into AC for household appliances. Solar power system efficiency and operation depend on inverter choice, grid-tied or off- grid.

Backup generators or other power sources are often used with off-grid solar power systems to provide electricity during poor sunshine or high energy demand. This hybrid solution addresses the intermittent nature of solar energy by providing reliable power. Backup power sources make off-grid systems more resilient and solve energy production and consumption issues.

Off-grid solar power systems offer several benefits, making sustainable, independent lifestyles appealing. Solar energy's environmental sustainability is a significant benefit. Solar power generates electricity without greenhouse gases or other pollutants. Environmentally responsible off-grid solar systems help people minimize their carbon footprint and fight climate change. The sun powers off-gridders' sustainable energy alternative, which protects the environment.

Cost savings and financial freedom are further benefits of using solar electricity off-grid. Despite high startup expenses, utility bill savings are substantial. Electricity costs drop for off-gridders, freeing up funds for other sustainable living. Solar power systems pay off over time, giving financial independence and lowering utility dependence. Government incentives and tax credits for renewable energy installations can further reduce upfront costs, making solar power systems an economically viable option for off-grid living.

Solar power systems reduce off-grid dependencies on external sources and grid infrastructure, improving energy resilience. Traditional power grids might fail owing to natural disasters, technical breakdowns, or other events. Solar power systems and energy storage allow off-grinders to sustain electricity supply during external disturbances. Resilience is vital in rural or off- grid areas with limited or no grid power. Off-grid solar systems protect residences from power outages.

Solar power systems are scalable and modular, allowing off-gridders to adapt their energy arrangements. Solar power systems can be expanded by adding solar panels, batteries, or inverters as energy needs rise. This flexibility allows lifestyle adjustments like adding appliances or expanding living areas. Solar power components are modular, making maintenance and upgrades easier. Off-grinders can retrofit or upgrade parts without replacing the whole system, making them flexible and adaptable to new technology.

Despite their many benefits, off-grid solar power systems have particular hurdles that must be overcome to maximize efficiency and reliability. Solar radiation varies throughout the day and season, making energy production difficult. For limited sunshine, strategic planning and energy storage are needed. Cloud cover, shadowing, and weather can affect solar panel performance. Off-grinders use generators and optimize energy during peak solar generation to overcome this issue.

An effective energy storage solution is needed to balance energy production and consumption. Batteries are essential for storing solar energy for usage in low-light conditions. Battery type, capacity, and maintenance affect off-grid solar power system performance. Off-grinders must carefully choose and maintain batteries to store energy and preserve power.

Location and orientation significantly affect solar panel efficiency. When choosing a place, off-grinders must consider average daily sunlight, seasonal fluctuations, and shading from adjacent structures or natural features. Understanding local sunlight conditions helps put and orient solar panels to maximum energy capture.

Off-grinders in northern latitudes may need to tilt their solar panels to maximize winter sunshine.

Off-grid solar power users must maintain and monitor their equipment. Solar panels are low-maintenance but need frequent inspections, cleaning, and repairs to perform well. Monitoring energy production, battery levels, and system health helps off-grinders spot and fix problems early. Proactive maintenance prolongs and optimizes the solar power system, making off-grid living sustainable and accessible.

In conclusion, solar power systems are revolutionizing off-grid life by providing a clean, reliable energy source. From photovoltaic panels to charge controllers, batteries, and inverters, off-grid solar systems allow people to generate, store, and use electricity. Solar power offers environmental sustainability, economic savings, energy resiliency, scalability, and modularity. It is an attractive and practical option for an independent and sustainable life. Off-grinders can harness the sun's power and live a more sustainable, self-sufficient, and separate existence despite sporadic sunshine and system maintenance.

Wind Energy Solutions

Wind energy, harnessed for ages, has a new function in off-grid life. As people look for renewable energy sources, wind energy is a robust and reliable option for off-grid electricity generation. Self-sufficient and environmentally conscious off-grinders use wind and solar electricity to power their homes. This section examines wind energy options in off-grid living, including wind turbine technology, wind power's pros and cons, and its transforming role in creating a sustainable and independent lifestyle.

Wind energy solutions rely on wind turbines, sophisticated machines that turn wind energy into electricity. An aerodynamic interaction between moving air and turbine blades is fundamental to wind turbine operation. Wind lifts the blades, rotating them. A generator converts mechanical energy into electricity from this circular action. Small household wind turbines to giant industrial turbines are available. The two primary types of turbines, horizontal and vertical, have different benefits and uses. Most people utilize horizontal-axis turbines with flat blades. Vertical-axis turbines are easy to maintain and suitable for urban or limited settings.

Wind energy options for off-grid living offer many benefits, making wind power a sustainable energy source. Wind turbines can create electricity even with little sunlight, which is a significant benefit. Wind energy can be used 24/7, making it a reliable and supplementary source of electricity in off-grid areas. Wind turbines provide reliable power in places with steady and moderate wind speeds. This dependability helps off-grid systems cope with changing energy output and consumption trends.

Wind energy is clean and renewable, promoting environmental sustainability. Wind power does not release greenhouse gases or air pollution. Off-grinders who use wind energy reduce their carbon footprint and climate change. Wind turbines symbolize responsible energy production, environmental conservation, and a cleaner, more sustainable future. Wind power in off-grid living reduces dependence on non-renewable resources and promotes eco-friendly alternatives.

Wind energy for off-grid living is attractive due to its affordability. Wind turbine systems have high startup costs but high long-term savings and ROI. After installation, wind turbines are cheap to operate and don't need fuel. Electricity bills drop for off-gridders, freeing up funds for other sustainable living. Due to government subsidies and tax rebates, wind power is economically viable for off-grid living.

Wind energy systems are scalable, allowing off-gridders to adapt to changing needs. Wind turbine systems can be expanded as energy needs rise by adding turbines or upgrading to larger ones. This flexibility enables lifestyle adjustments like adding appliances or expanding living areas. Wind energy components are modular, making maintenance and upgrades easier. Off-grinders can modify or replace turbines without redesigning the system, making them flexible and adaptable to new technology.

Off-grid wind energy solutions have many benefits but also present unique problems that must be overcome to maximize efficiency and dependability. Wind velocity can vary, making electricity generation difficult. Cut-in speed is the lowest wind speed needed for wind turbines to start rotating and generate power. They shut down at a maximum cut-out speed in heavy winds to prevent damage. To establish wind power viability and efficiency, off-gridders must thoroughly assess their location's wind potential. Strategic turbine location considers wind directions and topography to maximize energy capture.

Wind turbine noise and visual impact may affect nearby residents. Through advanced technology and blade designs, new wind turbines reduce noise, yet some may still find the hum or swishing sound disturbing. Large turbines may appear invasive in some locations; therefore, visual aesthetics matter. Off-grinders must weigh the benefits of wind power against its possible impact on their surroundings, considering their tastes and the local community.

Off-grid wind energy alternatives require ongoing turbine maintenance. Turbines are durable and reliable, but frequent inspections, lubrication, and problem-solving are necessary for maximum performance. Maintenance may involve blade wear, electrical component inspection, and safety feature testing. Proactive maintenance prolongs and optimizes the wind turbine system, making off-grid living easy. Wind energy alternatives for off-grid life depend on site selection. Off-gridders must carefully evaluate their location's wind resources.

Average wind speeds, prevalent wind directions, and local topography affect wind patterns. Meteorological agencies' wind maps and data can help site selectors choose places with constant and moderate wind speeds. Wind turbines should be placed in broad, unobstructed regions away from towering structures and natural features that can cause turbulence and hinder wind flow. Wind turbines are purposefully placed to maximize energy capture and system performance after a thorough site study.

Wind energy solutions transform off-grid living by providing clean, reliable, and scalable electricity. Off-grid wind power lets people generate, store, and use electricity by gracefully rotating turbine blades and integrating controls, inverters, and energy storage systems. Wind power appeals to independent and sustainable living enthusiasts due to its environmental sustainability, cost-effectiveness, energy resilience, scalability, and adaptability. Off-grinders can harness wind energy to live a more sustainable, self-sufficient, and independent lifestyle despite variable wind speeds, noise concerns, visual impact, maintenance, and site selection.

Hydro and Biomass Alternatives

Off-grid residents are using hydro and biomass energy sources to live sustainably. These energy alternatives use water and organic materials to give individuals seeking independence from power networks an edge. This section examines hydro and biomass alternatives for off-grid living, including their technology, benefits, and limitations.

For decades, renewable energy has relied on hydroelectric power, which uses water's kinetic energy. Micro-hydro systems provide scalable and reliable electricity in off-grid living, especially in regions with flowing water. Hydroelectric power converts potential energy in elevated water to kinetic energy as it descends, propelling a turbine to generate electricity. Micro-hydro systems range in capacity from modest installations for individual residences to enormous systems that power towns. Hydroelectric sites need enough water flow and a drop in height to capture energy.

Off-grid living benefits from hydroelectric power's consistency and predictability. River and stream flow is more stable than intermittent solar and wind power. This stability assures a steady power supply, making off-grid systems energy resilient. Micro-hydro systems provide off-grinders with clean, renewable, and environmentally sustainable energy in areas with sufficient water. Hydroelectric systems' scalability lets people customize their installations to meet their energy needs.

Site selection is crucial to micro-hydro system success. Off-gridders must evaluate their location's hydro potential, including water flow rates, elevation changes, and seasonal variations. Understanding local hydrology helps locate intake structures and turbines for optimal energy capture. Off-grid households use micro-hydro systems to generate electricity from on-site streams or rivers. Responsible off-grid hydroelectric project development requires site-specific considerations, including environmental impact evaluations and permitting.

Micro-hydro systems in off-grid life require careful design and maintenance. Off-grinders must evaluate their hydro systems due to water flow fluctuation, especially during droughts. Seasonal water level changes may require system design changes or other power sources during low-flow times. Maintaining sediment removal, debris management, and component structural integrity is crucial for micro-hydro system performance. Off-grinders must monitor and maintain their hydro installations to enhance efficiency and reduce environmental impact.

Wood, agricultural wastes, and animal manure can generate biomass energy for off-grid living. Heat from biomass combustion can be used for cooking, space heating, and electricity generation. Biomass energy is sustainable since combustion releases carbon dioxide into the carbon cycle. Off-grinders use local biomass like wood pellets, wood chips, and agricultural leftovers to generate energy sustainably. Additionally, biogas from organic waste provides a clean and renewable cooking and heating fuel.

The benefits of biomass energy in off-grid life go beyond its renewable nature. Biomass is generally local, minimizing energy imports. Off-grinders can use forestry, agriculture, and food production waste to conserve natural resources. Biomass energy is stable and available for off-grid living due to its decentralized nature. Biomass systems can generate power by gasification, anaerobic digestion, or direct burning in stoves or boilers.

Off-grinders who want a sustainable, abundant fuel source choose wood. Wood burners or biomass boilers efficiently heat and supply hot water for off-grid households using wood pellets or logs. Trees absorb carbon dioxide during growth, generating a carbon-neutral cycle. Sustainable forestry techniques like replanting and appropriate wood cutting preserve wood as a biomass supply for off-grid life.

Gasification allows off-grinders to generate electricity from biomass. Gasification turns biomass into flammable gas at high temperatures. This gas fuels internal combustion engines or generators, giving stable off-grid electricity. Off-grinders can diversify their energy portfolio using wood chips, crop residue, or other organic gasification devices.

Biogas from biological waste is a novel and sustainable off-grid living option. In anaerobic digestion, bacteria break down organic matter without oxygen, creating methane and carbon dioxide biogas. Biogas can be harvested for cooking, heating, and energy. Off-grinders can use small-scale anaerobic digesters to make biogas from food waste, agricultural residues, or animal manure, lowering fuel use and organic waste's environmental impact.

Biomass energy has many benefits, but off-grid life requires sustainable sourcing, combustion, and waste management. Responsible forestry emphasizes replanting and forest management to keep wood biomass renewable. Off-grinders must use clean, efficient combustion technology to reduce pollution and increase biomass energy output. Stoves, boilers, and gasification equipment need regular maintenance to work well and reduce air pollution. Ash leftovers from biomass burning must be managed to avoid soil pollution and environmental degradation.

Biogas systems are promising; however, organic waste availability and regularity are issues. When determining anaerobic digestion feedstocks, off-gridders must consider seasonal fluctuations, waste output rates, and organic material availability. To accommodate feedstock availability, digester and gas storage sizing must be correct. Proper digestate disposal or composting helps off-grid live biogas systems be used responsibly and sustainably.

In conclusion, hydro and biomass alternatives are adaptable and eco-friendly off-grid renewable energy choices. Flowing water powers hydroelectric systems, which generate energy reliably and consistently.

When properly planned and maintained, micro-hydro facilities boost the energy resilience of off-grid systems and provide renewable electricity—organic biomass energy powers off-gridders. Having the ability to heat, cook, and generate electricity locally. Wood, agricultural leftovers, and biogas are biomass options with different pros and downsides.

Hydro and biomass alternatives make off-grid life sustainable and self-sufficient, but site selection, system design, maintenance, and responsible sourcing are difficult. Hydro and biomass solutions must be integrated into off-grid lifestyles by rigorous research, local resources, and environmentally responsible activities. Off-grinders can use water and organic materials to create a more sustainable, resilient, and autonomous lifestyle.

CHAPTER IV

Water Independence

Rainwater Harvesting

People living off the grid are looking for creative ways to live sustainably and independently while making the most use of available resources. One particularly effective tactic is rainwater harvesting, which allows off- gridders to collect and store precipitation for various applications, such as drinking water and plant irrigation. The dynamics of rainwater contained in the context of off-grid living are examined in this section, along with the technology underlying rainwater collection systems, their advantages, and their revolutionary role in fostering an independent and sustainable way of life.

The essence of rainwater harvesting is to gather, store, and use rainwater that falls on roofs or other catchment surfaces. A rainwater collecting system includes a catchment area, conveyance system, storage tanks, filter, and distribution system. Rainwater is directed to gutters and downspouts from the collecting area, frequently a building's roof, which conveys the water to storage tanks. Rainwater collection systems, such as screens or filters, eliminate impurities and particles to guarantee the water's cleanliness for various uses. The off-grid home's distribution systems, fitted with pumps or gravity flow, transport the rainwater storage to its multiple locations.

The ability of rainwater harvesting to cover a variety of water needs is one of the main advantages of off-grid living. Off-grinders can lessen their reliance on traditional water sources by using collected rainwater for non-potable uses, including cleaning, toilet flushing, and irrigation. Furthermore, rainwater can function as a dependable and safe source of drinking water with the proper filtering and treatment techniques, giving off-grinders a self-sufficient water supply. Customizing rainwater collecting systems to meet individual requirements enables people to maximize water use in their off-grid living.

Rainwater harvesting's environmental sustainability is a strong argument in favor of conserving regional water supplies and lessening the adverse effects of water use on the environment. Off-grinders collect rainwater locally by collecting rainwater locally by reducing dependency on centralized water supplies, which may require energy-intensive water purification and delivery procedures. Rainwater collection promotes a more sustainable approach to water management by reducing the stress on nearby ecosystems, rivers, and aquifers. Maintaining natural water sources is especially important for off-grid living, where people want to live sustainably and leave as little ecological trace as possible.

In off-grid life, economic factors make rainwater harvesting even more appealing. Installing rainwater collecting systems can save money on water bills over time, especially in areas where water is expensive or scarce. The expenses of using conventional water sources are reduced or eliminated for off-gridders, freeing up cash for other sustainable living endeavors. The capacity to extend or alter configurations in response to fluctuating water demands is another benefit of the modularity and scalability of rainwater collecting systems, raising the effectiveness of this water management technique.

Rainwater harvesting provides a lifeline for off-gridders looking to develop resilient and self-sufficient lifestyles in areas where water shortage is a persistent concern. To prepare for dry seasons or droughts, off-gridders gather and store rainwater during periods of precipitation. This rainwater reserve acts as an essential buffer against variations in water availability, guaranteeing a steady water supply for necessities even when conventional water supplies can become limited or unstable. Rainwater collection offers water resilience consistent with off-grid living ideals, emphasizing readiness and self-sufficiency.

When living off the grid, collecting rainwater quality is crucial, mainly if the water will be used for drinking. To reduce the buildup of pollutants, the conveyance system and the collection surface—typically the roof—must be planned and maintained. The accumulation of debris, bird droppings, and other pollutants that could degrade the quality of rainfall collected is avoided by routinely cleaning gutters and downspouts. By eliminating contaminants before storage, filtration systems like fine mesh filters and first flush diverters improve water quality even more. Rainwater used for drinking may be treated with UV sterilization or other techniques to guarantee that it satisfies safety requirements.

Rainwater harvesting systems must be thoughtfully designed and maintained to protect water quality and enhance the health and welfare of off-gridders.
Although rainwater collection has many benefits, off-grid living presents difficulties due to the requirement for efficient system design, upkeep, and compliance with local laws. To reduce contamination and maximize water capture, great attention must be taken to the design of the conveyance system and catchment area. To find the most effective design for their particular requirements, off-gridders must evaluate the size and arrangement of their roofs, the kind of roofing materials, and the frequency of rainwater gathering. Installing screens, filters, and first flush diverters enhances storage tanks' longevity and water quality preservation. Rainwater harvesting systems must have regular maintenance to function dependably and efficiently. This maintenance must include cleaning the gutters, checking the components, and quickly addressing potential problems.

Off-grinders may have to deal with legal and regulatory issues about rainwater gathering in various areas. Rainwater collection and use are governed by water rights legislation or limits in some locations. To ensure compliance with legal requirements, off-grinders must be aware of local legislation and secure the relevant permissions or approvals. While off-grinders strive to promote a more comprehensive knowledge of rainwater gathering as a sustainable and responsible water management practice, advocacy and education may play a part in correcting out-of-date or prohibitive policies. One must engage with local authorities and water management agencies to navigate the legal environment and advance the acceptance of rainwater collection in off-grid life.

Educational programs and awareness campaigns

facilitate the adoption of rainwater collection in off-grid populations. Giving people access to knowledge about the advantages, appropriate design, and upkeep procedures enables them to decide whether to adopt rainwater harvesting into their lifestyle. Promoting a water conservation and self-sufficiency culture through workshops, community outreach initiatives, and online resources pushes off-grid lifestyle advocates to adopt sustainable water practices more widely. Off-grinders can aid the broader adoption of rainwater collection and its beneficial effects on water sustainability by exchanging information and experiences.

Rainwater collecting is a shining example of

sustainability and inventiveness in off-grid living. Through seizing and putting to use the liquid gold that rains from the sky, off-grinders can create robust, independent water systems that adhere to sustainability and environmental care. Reducing dependence on centralized water supply and lessening the effects of water shortages make rainwater harvesting adaptable and game-changing for those who want to live in peace with the environment. Difficulties with system design, upkeep, and legal implications highlight the significance of meticulous planning and community interaction. Off-grinders that embrace rainwater harvesting use precipitation to create a more independent, water-resilient, and sustainable way of life.

Well and Groundwater Management

People who want to live off the grid, where sustainability and self-sufficiency are crucial, frequently rely on wells and groundwater as their primary water supplies. Because well and groundwater management offers a dependable and dispersed water supply, they are vital in determining the water resilience of off-grid populations. In the framework of off-grid living, this section investigates the intricacies of managing groundwater and wells. It looks at the technology underlying well systems, their advantages, and the difficulties in using them sustainably.

When discussing off-grid life, a well is an artificial construction intended to access groundwater and underground aquifers. Water can flow naturally into the well by drilling or excavating a hole until reaching the water table. There are several different kinds of wells, such as driven, trained, and excavated. Each form of the well has a unique construction process and is appropriate for particular geological circumstances. How a well is designed and built is essential in influencing its sustainability, water quality, and efficiency. Groundwater management is a continuous duty for off-gridders once a well is installed, guaranteeing the sustainable use of this priceless resource.

The independence in obtaining water resources that well and groundwater management offer is one of the main advantages of off-grid life. Systems provide off-grinders with a decentralized and dependable water source, unlike centralized water supplies, which are vulnerable to infrastructure constraints and possible outages. The autonomy that wells offer is consistent with the ideas of off-grid living, which aims to lessen reliance on outside services and create robust, self-sufficient systems. Well water, extracted straight from underground aquifers, frequently needs no processing, which adds to the ease of use and long-term viability of off-grid water sources.

For off-grid communities, groundwater—the water kept below the earth's surface in porous rock formations, aquifers, and soil—represents a substantial and frequently unexplored resource. To ensure the sustainable use of this untapped resource, well and groundwater management involves a working knowledge of aquifer dynamics, regular monitoring of water levels, and the application of conservation measures. Natural processes like precipitation and infiltration replenish groundwater, but to avoid overexploitation, the extraction rate must be regulated with that of recharge. In off-grid living, well management measures such as appropriate well construction, routine maintenance, and conscientious water use all help to prolong and protect groundwater supplies.

Off-grid communities are more resilient when they have reliable and steady access to healthy water, particularly in areas where surface water supplies may be limited or unstable. Because underground aquifers shield groundwater from contamination and evaporation, ensuring a steady and safe water supply. Wells can provide off-grinders essential water for cooking, drinking, irrigation, and watering livestock. The systems' decentralized design enables people to customize their water use to meet particular demands, encouraging an adaptable and flexible approach to off-grid living.

To ensure that water is suitable for various uses, well and groundwater management involves monitoring and maintaining water quality. Because groundwater naturally filters itself as it seeps into the earth, it is typically considered an uncontaminated water source. However, regional geology, land use, and possible contaminants can all impact healthy water quality. Well-water testing is required of off-grinders for elements including pH, minerals, bacteria, and other potential pollutants. To address particular difficulties with water quality, filtration and treatment methods can be used to ensure the water is suitable for drinking and other household applications.

The management of wells and groundwater for off-grid living presents challenges due to the necessity for meticulous planning, upkeep, and environmental awareness. To protect the integrity of the water supply and avoid contamination, healthy construction must follow specified guidelines. Geological features, groundwater depth, and possible contamination sources are all considered while choosing good locations. Off- grinders must be mindful of local laws and secure required licenses before drilling or building a well. Regular good maintenance is necessary for best results and to avoid well-related concerns. This includes cleaning, disinfecting, and swiftly treating any problems.

A significant obstacle to well and groundwater

management is the over-extraction of groundwater, which can deplete aquifers and result in long-term water scarcity. Off-grinders are required to evaluate the wells' sustainable yield, considering variables like aquifer recharge rates and the well's ability to supply water without negatively affecting the environment. Adopting water-saving techniques, such as rainwater collection and adequate irrigation, encourages the sustainable use of this priceless resource and helps lessen dependency on healthy water. Periodic evaluation of groundwater levels is another aspect of sound management that ensures extraction rates don't surpass an aquifer's natural replenishment capability.

Environmental factors heavily influence groundwater and

healthy management since off-grid life strongly emphasizes living harmoniously with the environment. Wells need to be built and maintained to minimize their adverse effects on the environment and preserve ecosystems. Because excessive groundwater extraction can impact stream flows and riparian ecosystems' health, off-grinders should be aware of potential interactions between wells and surface water sources. The ecological sustainability of well and groundwater management in off-grid living can be enhanced by interacting with local environmental authorities, conducting in-depth site studies, and implementing responsible water use practices.

Due to climate variability and change, off-grid populations face additional issues in managing groundwater and wells. Extended droughts, harsh weather events, or changes in precipitation patterns can impact water availability and groundwater recharge rates. Off-grinders need to consider climate resilience when managing their wells; this includes considering things like the possibility of lower recharge during dry spells or the requirement for additional water sources during protracted droughts. Adaptive techniques that consider the dynamic character of water availability in shifting environmental conditions are part of climate-informed health management.

Effective well and groundwater management in off-grid life requires education and community involvement. Knowledge about healthy buildings, upkeep procedures, and conscientious water usage encourages environmental care and consciousness. Off-grinders are given the tools to manage their groundwater supplies and wells through joint projects, community engagement campaigns, and workshops. Individuals help to promote water resilience in off-grid areas by spreading sustainable well and groundwater practices through sharing their knowledge and experiences.

Water Filtration and Purification

Water is a vital resource for life and the main focus of off-grid living, where sustainability and self-sufficiency are critical. Off-grinders who want to be independent of centralized utilities frequently use water filtration and purification devices to provide a safe and clean water supply. The dynamics of water filtration and purification are examined in this section in the context of off-grid life, along with the technology underlying these systems, their advantages, and the difficulties in guaranteeing access to drinkable water in isolated and self-sufficient communities.

One of the main components of off-grid water management is water filtration, which is the process of purifying water of pollutants and impurities. Off-grinders frequently use various filtering techniques, from basic physical filters to more complex systems using mesh, ceramic, or activated carbon. The main objective is to filter away more prominent pollutants, silt, and particles to enhance the water's quality and visual clarity. The first line of defense is filtration, which keeps impurities out of the water supply and sets the stage for further purifying procedures.

On the other hand, water purification goes beyond water treatment by removing or rendering dangerous bacteria, viruses, and other possible pathogens inactive. Standard purification techniques include reverse osmosis, ultraviolet (UV) irradiation, and chemical disinfection. Every technique focuses on particular kinds of pollutants, offering a multi-barrier strategy to guarantee the elimination of various contaminants. Purification is essential for off-grinders who depend on natural water sources like wells, rivers, or rainfall, where microbial contamination may present health problems.

Decentralized and dependable water supplies are essential for off-grid life, which calls for efficient water filtration and purification technologies. These systems have numerous advantages that improve off-grid communities' sustainability, well-being, and general health. First of all, water filtration and purification enhance the quality of the water, guaranteeing off-grinders access to safe and clean drinking water. This feature is crucial to public health since contaminated water can harbor microorganisms that cause waterborne diseases. By implementing solid filtration and purification protocols, off-gridders protect their health and provide the groundwork for a robust and independent way of life.

Water filtration and purification systems provide independence from outside utilities, consistent with the off-grid lifestyle philosophy. Whether their water comes from wells, rivers, or rain catchment systems, off-grinders can customize their water treatment systems to meet the unique requirements of their water sources. This flexibility promotes a fluid and dynamic approach to off-grid water management by ensuring that water treatment solutions are tailored to the particular constraints provided by various water supplies.

Off-grid living places a high value on environmental sustainability, and water filtration and purification help ensure that water resources are used responsibly. Off-grinders lessen the influence on nearby ecosystems and their ecological footprint by efficiently purifying and recycling water. Water treatment systems frequently reroute their discharge into the environment in a way that reduces environmental damage. The preservation of this priceless resource is further aided by utilizing natural water sources and effective water management techniques like filtration and purification.

The adoption of water filtration and purification devices for off-grid life is also strongly influenced by cost. High-quality filtration and purification technologies can be expensive initially, but in the long run, they can save medical costs and prevent illnesses linked to contaminated water. Additionally, off-grinders save money and energy by reducing their reliance on bottled water or the need to transfer water from other sources. Many water purification systems have a long lifespan, which increases their cost-effectiveness and offers off-grid populations a viable and affordable option.

The variety of water sources and the fluctuation in water quality provide one of the main obstacles to off-grid water filtration and purification. Off-grinders need to evaluate the features of their unique water supply and adjust their treatment systems appropriately. Water can vary significantly in sediment, microbiological presence, and chemical composition, necessitating careful consideration when choosing filtration and purification techniques. Additionally, seasonal variations, weather patterns, or other environmental factors may cause changes in the water quality for off-gridders. To overcome these obstacles, off-gridders must treat water with a proactive and flexible strategy that involves constant system monitoring and adjustment to guarantee peak performance.

When treating water outside the grid, power source dependability is another factor. Reverse osmosis and other sophisticated filtration techniques like UV irradiation might need power. To provide a consistent and sustainable power supply for their water treatment systems, off-gridders need to incorporate alternative power sources like solar or wind energy. Furthermore, as off-grid communities work to reduce their overall energy use and maintain a balance between power generation and usage, the energy efficiency of water treatment technology becomes critical.

Maintenance is essential to guarantee the long-term efficacy of water filtration and purification systems. To maintain optimal performance, filtration media, such as ceramic or activated carbon filters, must be changed regularly. In disinfection systems, UV lights may eventually become less effective and must be replaced. Reverse osmosis membranes and filter housings, for example, require routine cleaning and sanitation to prevent the accumulation of impurities that could lower water quality. To avoid interruptions in the water supply, off-gridders need to be proactive in monitoring their water treatment systems, doing regular maintenance, and acting quickly to resolve any problems.

Water filtration and purification for off-grid life also involve chemical safety and waste management considerations. Chemicals like iodine or chlorine may be used in some purification processes to disinfect the water. Off-grinders must handle and store these chemicals securely, adhering to suggested practices to avoid unintentional exposure or contaminating the environment. Additionally, to reduce any possible environmental impact, proper waste management techniques must be followed when disposing of spent filtration media or purifying by-products. Including chemical-free or low-impact water treatment alternatives aligns with the sustainable and environmentally responsible off-grid living concepts.

In summary, water filtration and purification are essential for off-grid water management, giving self-sufficient communities access to dependable, safe, and clean water supplies. These systems' technology consists of various techniques and strategies designed to deal with particular problems from multiple water sources. Water treatment has several advantages for off-grid living, including cost-effectiveness, flexibility, environmental sustainability, and autonomy, in addition to health and safety. Variations in water quality, power sources, maintenance, chemical safety, and waste management are challenges that highlight the importance of meticulous planning, continual monitoring, and community involvement. Off-grinders can guarantee access to clean, clear waters and establish a robust, self-sufficient, and sustainable way of life by overcoming these obstacles.

CHAPTER V

Building Off-Grid Structures

Eco-Friendly Architecture

Eco-friendly design has become a transforming force in the goal of sustainable and ecologically conscious living, changing how people interact with their built environments. This section investigates the benefits, technologies, and guiding principles of eco-friendly architecture, highlighting this method of building and designing. Integrating energy-efficient technologies and using renewable materials make eco-friendly architecture a shining example of innovation that fosters coexistence between human habitation and the natural environment.

The cornerstone of eco-friendly architecture is

minimizing environmental effects through ethical design and building techniques. A vital component of this strategy is material selection, emphasizing locally obtained, repurposed, or renewable resources. Reclaimed materials, bamboo, recycled steel, and sustainable wood are used in environmentally friendly buildings, which lessens the need for virgin resources and the environmental impact of using conventional building materials. The durability and sustainability of eco-friendly structures are enhanced by using easily replenishable or reused materials.

One of the main principles of eco-friendly design is

energy efficiency, which addresses the significant environmental impact of energy use in the built environment. Building energy performance can be improved by implementing passive design principles, which include correct insulation, thermal mass usage, and carefully placed windows to allow for natural lighting and ventilation. Energy demands are decreased by integrating energy-efficient lighting, sophisticated HVAC systems, and high-performance windows. Eco-friendly structures occasionally use on-site renewable energy sources, like solar or wind turbines, to produce clean, sustainable power, advancing the concept of an increasingly resilient and self-sufficient energy system.

Because water supplies are limited, eco-friendly architecture strongly emphasizes water conservation and the need to use less water overall. Rainwater collecting systems, greywater recycling, and water-efficient fixtures reduce water use in eco-friendly buildings. Green design adheres to sustainability principles and lessens the demand on centralized water supply by collecting and reusing rainwater for irrigation or non-potable applications. By utilizing sensors and timers, intelligent irrigation systems enhance water efficiency in landscaping and support an all-encompassing strategy for water conservation.

Sustainable architecture is not limited to individual structures but includes community planning and design. Walkability, green spaces, and diverse land use are all integrated into sustainable urban design to produce places that maximize human well-being and reduce environmental damage. Green corridors, public transportation systems, and pedestrian-friendly walkways all help to build a feeling of community and lessen dependency on cars. Urban greening initiatives like parks, green roofs, and community gardens encourage biodiversity and improve people's quality of life.

Green building certifications, like BREEAM (Building Research Establishment Environmental Assessment Method) and LEED (Leadership in Energy and Environmental Design), provide a standard framework for evaluating and identifying sustainable building practices and as benchmarks for eco-friendly architecture. These certifications assess a building's energy efficiency, water conservation, indoor air quality, and use of environmentally friendly materials, among other design, construction, and operation factors. Architects and builders show their dedication to sustainability by following these certification criteria, which promote responsibility and openness in the building sector.

Eco-friendly architecture has advantages in the social and economic spheres and the environment. Energy-efficient buildings frequently have lower operating expenses throughout their lifetime since less energy used equals less utility bills. Furthermore, eco-friendly designs might be eligible for grants, tax credits, or other financial incentives that support sustainable building methods. Eco-friendly buildings are a good investment because of their long-term economic viability, which appeals to developers, businesses, and homeowners alike.

The focus eco-friendly architecture places on making buildings healthier and more habitable for their occupants clearly indicates its societal influence. Deliberate design components, improved indoor air quality, and access to natural light enhance the well-being of building residents. Including green areas and applying biophilic design ideas improves mental well-being and strengthens ties to the natural world. Eco-friendly neighborhoods encourage social cohesion, walkability, and a shared sense of environmental responsibility in community development.

Adopting environmentally friendly architecture is hampered by the initial expense of sustainable materials and technologies. Even though the long-term advantages frequently outweigh the upfront costs, some builders and homeowners may find the more considerable initial outlay a barrier. Furthermore, getting eco-friendly materials and technologies in some areas may be difficult. Thus, careful planning and sourcing are necessary to guarantee adherence to sustainable principles. To overcome these obstacles, the building sector must adopt a new perspective emphasizing the social value and long-term advantages of environmentally friendly architecture.

Innovation in environmentally friendly architecture is fueled by technological improvements, which create new opportunities for sustainable construction techniques. Innovative energy storage solutions, 3D printing for sustainable material construction, and intelligent building systems that optimize energy use based on occupancy patterns are examples of emerging technology. Buildings can respond to shifting environmental circumstances thanks to the integration of artificial intelligence (AI) and Internet of Things (IoT) technology, which improves energy efficiency and occupant comfort. As these technologies advance, they can completely change the field of environmentally friendly architecture by increasing the accessibility and scalability of sustainable practices.

An integral part of environmentally responsible architecture is resilient design, which recognizes the difficulties presented by climate change and the necessity of adjusting to changing environmental circumstances. Communities and buildings that are resiliently designed can tolerate harsh weather, temperature swings, and other climate-related effects. The total resilience of eco-friendly structures is increased by techniques like raised foundations, climate-responsive building envelopes, and green infrastructure, which guarantee the structures' operation and endurance in the face of climate change.

Globally, eco-friendly architecture is becoming more popular as people, companies, and governments realize how urgent it is to solve environmental issues. Green building certifications, energy efficiency requirements, and policies and legislation supporting sustainable building practices all help to make eco-friendly architecture more widely accepted. Financial incentives, including tax exemptions or subsidies for environmentally friendly buildings, promote adopting eco-friendly practices in the mainstream construction sector.

Promoting a general understanding of eco-friendly architecture and its advantages depends primarily on educational programs and awareness efforts. Information regarding available resources, technologies, and sustainable building techniques must be accessible to architects, builders, and customers. Conferences, workshops, and educational initiatives all support an ecosystem of knowledge exchange that enables stakeholders to make well-informed decisions that put environmental sustainability first.

To sum up, environmentally conscious architecture is a shining example of responsibility and creativity in the building sector, influencing the direction of sustainable living. An all-encompassing approach to building that places a premium on social, economic, and environmental sustainability is embodied by eco-friendly architecture, which uses resilient technologies, energy-efficient design principles, and renewable materials. By overcoming obstacles and embracing technology, eco-friendly design provides a way to create constructed environments that are in harmony with the natural world, improving occupant well-being and making the earth more resilient and sustainable.

Sustainable Building Materials

The need for sustainable building materials has emerged in the always-changing construction industry as a critical component of ethical and ecologically responsible design. This section explores the topic of sustainable building materials, highlighting the innovations, advantages, and guiding principles that support this vital facet of contemporary architecture. Sustainable building materials, which range from recycled to renewable resources, open the door for a construction sector that aligns with the demands of long-term resilience, ecological balance, and resource efficiency.

Sustainable building materials are fundamentally about minimizing the impact of construction on the environment through careful decision-making at every stage of the project's life cycle. Sustainable building practices are based on using renewable materials, which come from naturally occurring resources that are renewing quickly. Cork, bamboo, and timber from sustainably managed forests are excellent examples of renewable materials that support ethical forestry methods while providing strength, adaptability, and aesthetic appeal. Utilizing renewable resources ensures that raw material extraction is within the planet's potential for regeneration, consistent with resource conservation concepts.

Another aspect of sustainable building methods is using recycled and upcycled materials, which keep waste out of landfills and cut down on the demand for virgin resources. Construction projects give new life to recycled steel, reclaimed wood, and recycled glass, promoting the circular economy and reducing the environmental impact of raw material extraction and processing. Reusing materials allows for resource conservation and waste management by converting trash into valuable parts of solid, long-lasting constructions.

The latest technological advancements in sustainable building materials improve environmental friendliness and performance. Engineered wood products, such as cross-laminated timber (CLT) and laminated veneer lumber (LVL), demonstrate how sustainability and technology may coexist. These materials minimize the requirement for giant, mature trees by using smaller, quickly growing trees, offering excellent strength, durability, and dimensional stability. They advanced insulation materials that provide better thermal performance, such as aerogels and recycled cellulose, lower building energy use, and increase overall efficiency.

Energy-efficient building materials are essential to sustainable construction because they mitigate the significant environmental impact of structures' operational phases. Excellent roofing materials help save energy by lowering the demand for air conditioning in hot climates since they reflect more sunlight and absorb less heat than regular roofs. Similarly, intelligent glass technologies, including electrochromic or dynamic tinting, maximize natural light and temperature management while decreasing the need for artificial lighting and HVAC systems. Using energy-efficient building materials aligns with the overarching objective of developing structures that actively reduce greenhouse gas emissions and energy consumption.

By addressing issues with air quality and occupant well-being, sustainable building materials help to create healthier indoor spaces. Low-emission materials reduce the amount of potentially dangerous pollutants released into indoor air. Examples of these materials are low-VOC (volatile organic compound) paints, adhesives, and finishes. By limiting the use of artificial chemicals, natural materials like untreated wood and clay plasters improve the air quality within buildings. Given that people spend much time indoors, these factors are critical, highlighting the significance of designing environments that support comfort and health.

One of the most essential instruments for assessing how construction decisions will affect the environment is the life cycle assessment (LCA) of building materials. LCA considers the entire life cycle of a substance, starting with the extraction and processing of raw materials and continuing through manufacturing, shipping, usage, and finally disposal or recycling. Through the evaluation of elements like embodied energy, greenhouse gas emissions, and resource depletion, life cycle assessment

(LCA) offers a thorough grasp of the environmental impact related to various construction materials. Using a holistic approach gives stakeholders, architects, and builders the ability to make well-informed decisions that prioritize sustainability over a building's entire life cycle.

Sustainable building materials are chosen to create long-lasting structures in mind, in addition to environmental considerations. A critical factor in sustainable building is durability, which reduces the need for regular upkeep, fixes, or replacements. Structures last longer when made of highly resistant materials to weathering, corrosion, and pests. This reduces the amount of additional resources needed for repairs or reconstruction. The overarching objective of developing resilient and adaptive buildings that can resist the difficulties presented by a changing climate and environmental circumstances is also aligned with using durable materials.

Although using sustainable building materials has many advantages, there are still obstacles to its general acceptance. For builders and developers, the upfront costs of certain sustainable materials could be a deterrent, especially in areas where financial concerns predominate when making construction decisions. Furthermore, some sustainable resources might not be readily available in some areas, necessitating considerable preparation and cooperation to guarantee a trustworthy supply chain. To overcome these obstacles, the construction industry must adopt a new perspective and acknowledge the social and long-term advantages of funding sustainable building techniques.

Certifications and regulatory frameworks are critical factors in encouraging the incorporation of sustainable building materials into conventional construction methods. Construction norms and standards that promote or require sustainable materials help normalize ecologically conscious building practices. A consumer's and the industry's clear signal regarding the sustainability credentials of particular building materials comes from certifications like the Cradle to Cradle CertifiedTM designation for materials designed for circularity or the Forest Stewardship Council (FSC) certification for wood sourced responsibly. Architects and builders help to elevate the bar for sustainable construction methods by adhering to set criteria.

Promoting sustainable building methods requires concerted efforts in education and awareness. Information regarding the advantages, traits, and accessibility of sustainable building materials must be made available to architects, builders, and customers. Workshops, conferences, and instructional initiatives support an ongoing learning and creativity culture by being part of an ecosystem that exchanges knowledge. The construction sector can expedite the shift towards more sustainable and responsible building practices by providing stakeholders with the necessary expertise.

To sum up, sustainable building materials are crucial in developing contemporary construction, providing a route towards robust and ecologically conscious buildings. Sustainable materials are integral to a construction process considering social, economic, and environmental aspects. They range from innovative technologies that improve performance to renewable and recycled resources. By overcoming obstacles and adopting life cycle assessment, energy efficiency, and durability as guiding principles, the construction sector can build for the future and produce environmentally conscious buildings that serve as examples of what is possible regarding sustainable living.

DIY Construction Tips

Starting a do-it-yourself (DIY) building project is an exciting adventure that enables people to customize their living areas to fit their needs and vision. The spirit of do-it-yourself construction is in the imagination, ingenuity, and the sense of accomplishment that comes from finishing a project by hand, no matter how big or small. This section examines many do-it-yourself construction pointers to help enthusiasts who are ready to take on the job of creating or remodeling their own spaces.

Careful planning is essential to effective do-it-yourself building. Outlining the project's scope, budget, and timetable is crucial before getting started. A well-thought-out strategy helps anticipate obstacles, prepare for unforeseen events, and act as a roadmap. Planning should consider required permissions, material pricing, and availability of tools and equipment. Devoting sufficient time to investigating and comprehending the project's demands comprehensively facilitates a more seamless construction process and increases the probability of a favorable result.

Safety is crucial when it comes to do-it-yourself construction. Setting safety precautions as a top priority guarantees no mishaps or injuries during construction. Gloves, safety glasses, and strong shoes are examples of personal protection equipment (PPE) that should be worn at all times. Learning how to handle tools and equipment correctly, following manufacturer instructions and suggested safety procedures, is essential. Keeping the workspace tidy and orderly also reduces the possibility of mishaps and promotes re-productivity. Detect potential hazards and put preventive measures in place; a complete risk assessment should be carried out before beginning any construction activity.

Choosing the right tools is essential when doing do-it-yourself building. An organized toolbox is like having a trustworthy partner for the duration of the job. Any toolbox must start with crucial hand tools like tape measures, pliers, screwdrivers, and hammers. Drills, saws, and sanders are examples of power tools that improve accuracy and efficiency. When purchasing tools, quality should come before quantity. Long-term returns on investment are achieved by purchasing sturdy and dependable instruments that can handle the rigors of various tasks. Tools operate better and last longer when they are correctly maintained and stored.

The ability to comprehend and handle building materials is essential for any do-it-yourself project to be successful. A fundamental understanding of the qualities of various materials is crucial because they each have unique uses and qualities. For example, metal may need to be rust-proof, whereas wood is adaptable but needs to be protected from dampness. Making educated selections during the planning and construction stages is facilitated by being familiar with the characteristics of various materials. Furthermore, investigating eco-friendly and sustainable materials aligns with modern building practices that place a premium on environmental responsibility.

The exact construction work is based on precise measurements. Accurate measurements must be taken before cutting, assembling, or installing items. Accuracy is ensured using high-quality measuring instruments like squares and tape measures. Verifying dimensions twice before cutting or installing anything will help you avoid expensive errors and rework. Accurate measurement from the beginning of a project pays off throughout construction, resulting in a final product that fulfills requirements and expectations.

Working with many trades is common in do-it-yourself building, and learning new skills expands the range of projects you may take on. While certain activities might require specialized training, hobbyists can learn and become proficient in many construction elements. Community programs, workshops, and online tutorials are excellent tools for learning new skills. Developing a foundation of varied talents allows one to do more do-it-yourself projects and promotes self-sufficiency and a sense of accomplishment.

One essential element of do-it-yourself construction is efficient time management. Setting attainable objectives and benchmarks is made more accessible by developing a realistic schedule. To avoid feeling overwhelmed and to guarantee consistent development, the project should be divided into smaller tasks and scheduled appropriately. It's critical to account for unforeseen delays and set aside more time for complex assignments or picking up new skills. Reevaluating the timeframe regularly and making necessary adjustments make construction go more smoothly and reduce stress.

Adaptability and flexibility are excellent traits in the realm of do-it-yourself building. Projects sometimes proceed more precisely as expected, and unanticipated difficulties might appear. Overcoming challenges requires the capacity to adjust to changing conditions, troubleshoot problems, and consider alternate solutions. DIY builders can overcome obstacles with resiliency and innovation and transform failures into chances for growth if they keep an optimistic and adaptable outlook.

Creating a support system is crucial for do-it-yourselfers. A supportive ecosystem is made by asking friends, fellow builders, or online groups for advice, direction, and opportunities for collaboration. Sharing thoughts, advice, and experiences creates a sense of unity and yields insightful information. Furthermore, getting assistance can significantly speed up the building process and improve the whole do-it-yourself project experience.

Budgeting and financial planning are essential components of do-it-yourself building. A realistic budget facilitates decision-making on supplies, equipment, and other project-related costs. It's critical to investigate and contrast expenses, look into affordable options, and budget for unforeseen costs. Following the budgetary restrictions reduces the possibility of going beyond and guarantees that the do-it-yourself project will stay financially viable.

Recording the building process with pictures, notes, or a project journal is a good idea. It functions as a record of the trip and a resource for upcoming initiatives or advancements. By recording the building process, essential insights such as effective methods, lessons discovered, and potential areas for development can be obtained. By making the documentation available to other members of the do-it-yourself community, you can expand their knowledge base and promote a collaborative learning culture.

Using sustainability in do-it-yourself building aligns with the public's increasing understanding of environmental responsibility. Choosing sustainable solutions, reusing materials, and recycling waste all help to make buildings more environmentally friendly. Including passive design principles, investigating energy-efficient technology, and taking the materials' life cycle impact into account are some approaches to including sustainability in do-it-yourself projects. By implementing eco-friendly strategies, do-it-yourself builders can achieve a more sustainable and environmentally friendly built environment.

To sum up, creating a home with your hands is an adventure in creativity, empowerment, and skill development. DIY enthusiasts can start effective and rewarding construction projects by combining careful planning, safety precautions, high-quality tools, material understanding, and an attitude of continual learning. DIY construction is fulfilling because of the practical skills learned along the road and the thrill of seeing a vision realized. The realm of do-it-yourself construction is open to people willing to take on the challenge of artistically and imaginatively designing and molding their living spaces, whether it's a minor home repair job or a larger-scale building project.

CHAPTER VI

Sustainable Food Production

Organic Gardening Techniques

Organic gardening has become popular as a comprehensive and environmentally responsible method of growing plants in a society with increasing awareness of environmental sustainability and conscious living. To help gardeners cultivate healthy, thriving plants while reducing their environmental impact, this section explores the concepts, practices, and advantages of organic gardening approaches.

An understanding of and dedication to cooperating with the cycles and systems of nature is fundamental to organic gardening. Organic gardening emphasizes sustainable methods and natural processes more than conventional gardening, which frequently uses artificial pesticides, fertilizers, and herbicides. In addition to producing an abundance of wholesome crops, the objective is to preserve water, promote biodiversity, and improve soil health. Organic gardening is a regenerative technique meant to restore the soil to its previous state of fertility and resilience.

Building and maintaining nutritious soil is fundamental in organic gardening, as soil health is paramount. Organic gardeners emphasize natural additions like compost, well-rotted manure, and cover crops over synthetic fertilizers. These inputs improve soil structure and microbial activity and give plants nutrients. Crop rotation is one technique that helps prevent the depletion of certain nutrients and reduces the danger of soil-borne diseases; it is one way that soil health is prioritized. Organic gardeners lay the basis for vigorous plant growth by cultivating a living and active soil environment.

The foundation of organic gardening is composting, which turns garden and kitchen waste into nutrient-rich humus. A natural fertilizer, compost strengthens soil structure, increases water retention, and encourages healthy microbial activity. Organic gardeners compost piles or bins from kitchen scraps, yard waste, and other organic elements. Microorganisms break down organic matter throughout the composting process, creating a beneficial soil amendment that is both economical and environmentally benign. Composting closes the circle in the garden ecosystem by recycling organic waste and lowering the need for outside inputs.

In organic gardening, companion planting is a planned method that capitalizes on the natural connections between several plant types. Gardeners create an atmosphere that is harmonious and supports the health of their plants by choosing plants that complement one another in terms of growth patterns, nutrient requirements, and insect resistance. For instance, placing fragrant herbs like basil close to tomatoes can aid in keeping pests away that frequently harm tomato plants. In addition to helping with pest control, companion planting optimizes the garden's effective use of resources and space.

An essential component of organic farming is biological pest control, which emphasizes using beneficial insects, parasites, and natural predators to control pest populations. Those who cultivate organically promote the presence of predators such as ladybugs, lacewings, and predatory beetles rather than using chemical pesticides that might destroy beneficial insects and upset the ecological balance. A biodiverse habitat that naturally controls pest populations can be created by planting flowers that draw pollinators and beneficial insects. Insecticidal soaps and the introduction of beneficial nematodes can also aid in managing particular pests without endangering the general health of the garden.

In organic gardening, crop diversification is essential for resilience and sustainability. Cultivating a single crop across vast areas, known as monoculture, exposes farmers to pest and disease outbreaks and may necessitate high inputs of synthetic chemicals. Organic gardeners, on the other hand, welcome polyculture and plant a range of crops that complement one another and help maintain a healthy ecology. In addition to increasing biodiversity and drawing a variety of helpful insects, diverse plantings make a garden more adaptable to natural shocks.

Organic gardening strongly emphasizes water conservation, and strategies like mulching and adequate irrigation reduce the amount of water used. Applying a layer of organic material to the soil's surface, or mulching, controls temperature, retains moisture, and inhibits weed growth. Organic gardeners use mulch made of straw, leaves, or compost to build a protective layer that holds soil moisture and lessens the need for regular watering. Drip irrigation systems reduce water waste and encourage effective water use in the garden by providing water straight to the base of plants.

A long-standing organic gardening tradition, seed saving helps to preserve heirloom types and strengthens the bond between gardeners and the plants they raise. Organic gardeners gather and maintain their plant seeds rather than depend exclusively on bought seeds every growing season. In addition to preserving genetic diversity, this gradually helps plants adjust to their particular growth environment. Seed saving is a sustainable gardening technique that encourages food self-sufficiency and equips gardeners to protect biodiversity.

Beyond the garden bed, organic gardening involves the prudent use of materials and resources. Designing a garden sustainably considers elements like utilizing recycled or repurposed materials, conserving electricity, and optimizing water usage. An eco-friendly garden can be created using rainwater collection systems, solar-powered garden lights, and repurposed materials. Organic gardeners go beyond simple plant care to demonstrate their commitment to sustainability by using eco-friendly techniques in garden design and upkeep.

The organic gardening movement is centered around education and community involvement. Online forums, community gardens, and workshops offer venues for exchanging best practices, insights, and experiences. Organic gardeners aid the promotion of sustainable and regenerative techniques by cultivating a culture of learning and cooperation. Sharing concepts and knowledge enables people to make sensible decisions, implement efficient methods, and encourage others to adopt organic gardening.

The advantages of organic gardening go beyond the garden's boundaries to include wider ecological and social effects. Organic gardens support pollinators, beneficial insects, and soil bacteria since they don't use synthetic chemicals and create a biodiverse ecosystem. This ecological resilience fosters a more sustainable interaction between humans and the environment and adds to the general health of ecosystems. Furthermore, by producing nutrient-dense, chemical-free vegetables, organic gardening can improve food security, lessen the environmental impact of agriculture, and foster healthier communities.

In summary, organic gardening methods represent a comprehensive and sustainable approach to plant cultivation, balancing with the environment to produce robust and colorful garden ecosystems. The fundamentals of organic gardening provide a road map for gardeners looking to grow in harmony with nature, covering everything from soil health and composting to companion planting, biological pest management, and water saving. As the movement gains traction, organic gardening transcends from a simple plant-growing technique to a philosophy that acknowledges the interdependence of all living things and aims to build a more sustainable, healthy future for people and the environment.

Permaculture Principles

Derived from the words "permanent agriculture" or "permanent culture," permaculture encompasses much more than just gardening and farming methods. It's a holistic design strategy based on ideas that support regenerative and sustainable living. This section examines the fundamental concepts of permaculture and the philosophy that directs practitioners in building robust systems that promote plenty, biodiversity, and harmony with the natural world.

The guiding concept of permaculture is to "observe and interact." Permaculturists observe any terrain's underlying patterns and processes before making changes or designing a system. Good design starts with understanding a location's particulars, such as its terrain, climate, and current ecosystems. By emphasizing the value of careful observation and interaction with the environment, this approach enables designers to collaborate with natural cycles rather than fight against them.

A cornerstone of permaculture is to "catch and store energy." This entails effectively capturing and using energy resources inside a system. In agriculture, it can take the form of using water catchment systems to collect rainwater for later use or carefully placing plants to trap sunlight. To promote resilience and adaptation within a design, permaculture considers factors other than physical energy, such as gathering and storing resources and information. Through optimizing the capture and storage of various energy types, permaculture systems achieve increased self-sufficiency and sustainability.

The idea of "obtain a yield" emphasizes how applicable permaculture is. Each component of a design needs to enhance the system's overall productivity. A key element of permaculture is the importance of tangible and valuable yields, be they knowledge, fuel, food, or fiber. This idea motivates practitioners to create systems that satisfy the needs of people and communities and promote ecological health. Permaculture cultivates a more sustainable and equitable approach to land usage by providing quantifiable yields and numerous purposes for each element.

"Apply self-regulation and accept feedback" recognizes that systems are dynamic and that ongoing adaptation is necessary. Permaculturists understand that designs must be modified over time in response to input from the community or the environment. This idea promotes a thoughtful and adaptable way of thinking, which builds resilience in the face of change. It highlights how crucial it is to preserve an equilibrium between inputs and outputs to stop resource depletion and reduce adverse environmental effects. Permaculture systems can change and adapt throughout time because of feedback loops and self-regulation.

"Use and value renewable resources and services" is consistent with sustainability's central idea. Prioritizing renewable resources above non-renewable ones and leveraging ecosystem services to improve resilience are vital components of permaculture. Practitioners can limit their adverse effects on the environment by choosing plant species that are well-adapted to the local area or including renewable energy sources in designs. Permaculture encourages a regenerative relationship with the Earth by valuing the benefits that natural systems give highly.

"Produce no waste" reflects permaculture's dedication to completing material cycle loops. Waste is a term that is primarily nonexistent since one system's outputs become another system's inputs. Permaculture designs use waste materials as valuable resources to replicate this closed-loop methodology. Waste is reduced by recycling, mulching, and composting inside the system. This idea pushes practitioners to reconsider waste, seeing it as a resource that can be used rather than as an issue that needs to be solved.

"Design from patterns to details" promotes a design

process incorporating systems thinking. Permaculturists begin by recognizing and comprehending more enormous patterns and linkages in the landscape instead of starting with individual pieces. Designers can produce more harmonious and well-integrated systems by identifying overarching patterns, such as wind direction, sunshine, and water movement. This idea encourages a comprehensive viewpoint, guaranteeing that a design's specifics fit into larger patterns and add to the system's overall harmony.

"Integrate rather than segregate" highlights the

essential interactions and linkages inside a system. Diversity is embraced in permaculture, and components are arranged purposefully to promote positive interactions. This idea opposes the traditional method of separating components and promotes combining various parts to produce synergy. For instance, planting multiple crops can have reciprocal advantages like increased yields, nutrient cycling, and insect control. Permaculture designs optimize the resilience and efficiency of the system as a whole by encouraging linkages.

The phrase "Use small and slow solutions" resists the

need for instant cures and promotes methodical, incremental approaches to problem-solving. Small-scale, gradual interventions are frequently more successful and long-lasting in permaculture than large-scale, abrupt ones. This idea recognizes the intricacy of natural systems and the value of tracking changes in those systems over time. Permaculture designs help to avoid unintended consequences and encourage the development of robust, resilient systems by allowing for incremental alterations and starting small.

"Use and value diversity" recognizes ecosystems' power in diversity. Diversity is seen as a significant factor in permaculture's resilience and productivity. To improve the general health and stability of the system, this principle encourages introducing a range of plants, animals, and microorganisms. Diverse systems offer a more excellent range of yields, are more resilient to pests and diseases, and can adjust to changing environmental conditions. Permaculture designs mimic the resilience inherent in natural ecosystems by appreciating and fostering diversity.

"Use edges and value the marginal" acknowledges the unique opportunities that arise at the points where various system elements converge. When referring to ecology, the edge is frequently a region of higher productivity and biodiversity. Recognizing that edges have the potential to boost yields, diversity, and efficiency, permaculture designs purposefully include them. This idea urges practitioners to focus on marginal regions and transitional zones, where many components interact. Maximizing the advantages of edges makes permaculture systems more versatile and dynamic.

The phrase "creatively use and respond to change" acknowledges that change is inevitable and challenges professionals to see it as a chance for creativity and adaptation. Permaculturists understand that systems are constantly changing and that designs need to be adaptable enough to consider these changing conditions. This idea encourages innovative thinking that views change as a necessary component of the design process. Permaculture designs may survive uncertainty and changing environmental dynamics by fostering resilience and flexibility.

To sum up, the principles of permaculture provide a thorough framework for creating regenerative systems that actively improve the health of the Earth beyond what is sustainable. Permaculturists build designs that work with nature, not against it, by embracing intelligent and perceptive techniques. By implementing these ideas, people can make more harmonious relationships with the environment and promote sustainability, abundance, and resilience for future generations. Individuals, communities, and societies can all benefit from this.

Raising Livestock and Poultry

Raising cattle and poultry is a long-standing agricultural tradition that yields valuable commodities like dairy, eggs, meat, and other byproducts. With the world changing so quickly and our awareness of health, environmental, and ethical issues growing, it is essential to consider the practices used in animal husbandry. The many facets of rearing cattle and poultry are examined in this section, which also explores the practical, ethical, and environmental elements of this intricate and necessary activity.

The dedication to moral treatment and care of animals is the cornerstone of ethical animal husbandry. Ensuring the humane care of cattle and poultry involves several aspects, such as providing sufficient space, nutritious feed, and uncontaminated water sources. In addition to avoiding needless stress and cruelty, ethical considerations also include the use of substances that promote growth. The Five Freedoms—freedom from hunger and thirst, discomfort, pain, injury, or disease, freedom to exhibit regular activity, and freedom from fear and distress—are the focal points of contemporary approaches to animal welfare. Ethical animal husbandry prioritizes the welfare of the animals, which is consistent with society's ideals and helps provide more sustainable and healthier food sources.

An essential component of adequate animal husbandry is selecting the correct species of livestock or poultry. Different animals have different requirements, traits, and environmental adaptability. Pigs could need a more regulated habitat, but cattle, for example, are better suited for pasture grazing. Known for their adaptability, chickens can be raised in agriculture for eggs, meat, or pest management. The proper species must be chosen after considering factors, including the operation's desired goal, market demand, climate, and available area. Farmers can maximize output and welfare by selecting animals that fit the farm's objectives and resources.

The productivity and well-being of cattle and poultry are significantly influenced by how they are housed and managed. Intensive confinement systems have been a common feature of conventional operations, which has raised concerns regarding animal welfare, environmental impact, and disease transmission. Alternative approaches that emphasize providing natural surroundings where animals can show their essential characteristics include pasture-based or free-range operations. Animals can access outside areas in pasture-based systems, encouraging foraging, exercise, and a more natural way of life. These technologies contribute to developing tasty, nutrient-dense goods while improving animal welfare.

Sustainable and regenerative farming approaches emphasize livestock integration into varied farming systems. For example, agroecology uses the complementary roles of crops and animals to acknowledge their symbiotic relationship. Livestock benefits from access to various forages and offers essential services such as weed control, nitrogen cycling, and soil enhancement. Rotational grazing systems with livestock integration improve soil health, lessen dependency on synthetic fertilizers, and increase overall farm resilience. Farmers may better enhance animal happiness and the health of their ecosystems by utilizing the natural behaviors of their livestock by considering them as essential elements of a holistic farming approach.

In the production of cattle and poultry, feed management is an essential factor that affects the animals' health, growth, and environmental effects. Concentrated feeds, such as soy and corn, are frequently used in conventional feeding procedures. These techniques can potentially worsen environmental degradation, monoculture, and deforestation. Locally produced and diverse feed resources are prioritized in sustainable alternatives, including agroecological techniques and pasture-based systems. The ecological impact of animal husbandry can be decreased by including cover crops, fodder, and leftovers from other agricultural operations. Furthermore, investigating novel feed alternatives like algae or insect protein could result in more sustainable and nutritionally balanced cattle diets.

A vital component of a profitable livestock and poultry operation is animal health. Preventative steps aid in preserving the health of the herd or flock and include immunization, parasite management, and biosecurity procedures. In addition to ensuring that animals are treated humanely, proactive health management boosts output and financial stability. Organic and sustainable agriculture aligns with integrating holistic and natural health methods, such as rotating grazing to disrupt parasite cycles or using herbal supplements. Producers can decrease their dependency on antibiotics and chemical interventions and increase the long-term viability of their operations by putting animal health first.

Programs for breeding and genetic selection impact the features and attributes of poultry and cattle. Characteristics including quick growth, high milk or egg production, and disease tolerance have frequently been given priority in conventional breeding. Although these characteristics could increase output, they may also have unforeseen drawbacks, such as decreased genetic diversity and higher susceptibility to specific illnesses.

The main goals of sustainable breeding methods are to maintain genetic variety, resilience, and environmental adaptability. Programs for the conservation of uncommon or heritage breeds help save distinctive genetic resources and promote biodiversity in the agricultural environment.

An essential component of ethical livestock and poultry production is animal waste management. Large volumes of manure are frequently produced by conventional concentrated animal feeding operations (CAFOs), which presents environmental problems like nutrient runoff, water pollution, and greenhouse gas emissions. Using animal dung as a valuable resource efficiently is prioritized in sustainable techniques. Manure can be efficiently managed by using anaerobic digestion, composting, or rotational grazing systems, which can turn it into soil conditioner, organic fertilizer, or biogas for energy. Producers may reduce their adverse effects on the environment and promote a more circular and regenerative approach to agriculture by seeing animal waste as an essential part of the farming system.

Certifications and standards for animal welfare offer a framework for evaluating and enhancing the care given to poultry and cattle. Criteria for moral and compassionate animal agricultural practices are set by several organizations, including the Certified Humane label and the Animal Welfare Approved (AWA) program. These guidelines address antibiotic use, outdoor area access, and housing circumstances. In addition to meeting customer expectations for humane treatment, producers who adhere to recognized welfare standards help the sector evolve toward more sustainable and ethical models.

Raising animals and poultry involves ethical issues that arise throughout the processing and killing phases. Conventional industrial slaughterhouses have come under fire for things including animal stress, harsh treatment, and unhygienic environments. The application of compassionate handling techniques, stunning procedures, and the provision of cozy holding areas are given top priority in ethical slaughtering operations. Local, smaller-scale abattoirs could provide options that meet ethical standards and encourage a more open, neighborhood-focused meat processing method. Furthermore, addressing ethical issues with conventional livestock production, the developing field of cultured or lab-grown meat offers a potential paradigm shift in animal agriculture.

Consumer understanding and decision-making greatly influence the environment surrounding moral and sustainable animal husbandry. Customers are becoming picky about products with labels suggesting organic certification, pasture-based systems, or ethical treatment. Producers have been forced to adopt more humane and sustainable procedures due to this demand, which has changed industry standards. Customers can help create a more sustainable food supply by selecting beef, dairy, and egg suppliers with knowledge.

Producing cattle and poultry requires striking a careful balance between environmental sustainability, practicality, and ethical issues. A commitment to humane treatment, an awareness of the various species' needs, and the careful integration of animals into farming systems are all necessary for responsible animal husbandry. The ever-changing world of livestock and poultry production necessitates a conscious and comprehensive approach as we traverse the complexity of modern agriculture—one that takes the well-being of the animals, the health of the environment, and the ethical implications of our decisions into consideration. For the good of everybody, farmers and consumers alike can support a more resilient and peaceful food system by adopting sustainable and regenerative practices.

CHAPTER VII

Waste Management

Composting Systems

An excellent way to manage waste and improve soil is by composting, a natural process that turns organic waste into nutrient-rich soil additives. Although composting is an art and science with deep origins in agricultural traditions, its importance has recently spread to backyard gardens, urban areas, and farmsteads. This section examines several composting methods, highlighting the critical role that composting plays in advancing environmental sustainability while also exploring the mechanics, advantages, and uses of each system.

Fundamentally, composting turns organic resources into a valuable soil conditioner through microbially-driven breakdowns. When bacteria, fungi, and other decomposers break down complex organic substances into simpler forms, magic happens. By creating the perfect environment for these microbes to flourish, composting systems transform yard waste, kitchen scraps, and other organic materials into what is frequently described as "black gold" for the soil.

The compost bin in the backyard or at home is one of the most accessible and popular composting solutions. With the help of this technology, people can recycle organic wastes such as yard clippings and kitchen garbage in a restricted area. Compost bins for the backyard range in style from straightforward covered bins to intricate tumblers that allow for easier rotation and aeration. Success requires careful layering of materials rich in carbon and nitrogen (brown), turning occasionally, and controlling moisture. Composting at home provides nutrient-rich compost that can be utilized to improve soil fertility in landscaping and gardens and keep organic waste out of landfills.

Composting using worms, also known as vermicomposting, is a particular kind of composting that uses the digestive capabilities of specific worm species, most commonly red wigglers or Eisenia fetida. Worms eat organic materials in a vermicomposting system, breaking them down into nutrient castings. Since they are frequently compact, vermicomposting containers are ideal for indoor or small-space composting. A consistent supply of kitchen scraps, moisture, and bedding materials must all be carefully balanced for these systems to function. Vermicompost, also known as worm compost or worm castings, is highly valued for its high microbial content and works wonders as a soil conditioner to improve plant health and growth.

Compared to conventional composting techniques, hot composting, often called thermophilic composting, is a quicker and more heat-intensive process. The microbial activity in hot composting systems raises the temperature to lethal levels for diseases and weed seeds. To reach and sustain these high temperatures, the compost pile must be carefully tended, with appropriate rotation and aeration. Larger-scale companies, farms, or community composting projects are good candidates for hot composting. For individuals looking for a quicker composting procedure, the resultant compost is fully broken down and frequently ready for use in less time.

Digging organic waste and depositing it straight in the garden soil is a straightforward and discreet process known as trench composting. This technique entails preparing the soil by excavating trenches or furrows in the garden, then adding organic items such as cooking scraps and covering them with dirt. The buried organic matter breaks down over time, improving the soil and giving neighboring plants nutrition. Composting in trenches helps enhance garden beds' fertility and soil structure. It is a practical choice for individuals who would instead compost in-ground without requiring particular compost bins.

Anaerobic fermentation, or bokashi composting, has its roots in Japan. In this technique, bran—a blend of bran, molasses, and beneficial microorganisms—assists in the fermentation of kitchen waste. Because fermentation occurs inside an airtight container, organic materials can decompose without needing oxygen. The benefit of bokashi composting is that it can handle a variety of kitchen wastes, such as meat and dairy products, which would not be appropriate for conventional composting systems. After the trash has been fermented, it is usually placed in a traditional compost container or buried in the ground to finish the decomposition process.

Large-scale or industrial composting systems serve municipalities, waste management facilities, and agricultural activities handling large amounts of organic waste. For these systems to process vast amounts of organic material effectively, sophisticated equipment like windrow management and compost turners are frequently needed. Facilities for industrial composting are built to accommodate a variety of inputs, such as food scraps, yard trash, and agricultural leftovers. After processing appropriately, the resulting compost can be added to commercial soil blends or utilized for soil repair and erosion prevention.

Composting has several advantages beyond just turning organic waste into a valuable soil supplement. Reduced and diverted garbage is one of the main benefits. Individuals and groups can reduce the waste they send to landfills by composting organic materials. This will help mitigate the environmental effects of landfill decomposition, methane emissions, and limited landfill space. By recycling organic products back into the soil, composting helps close the natural nutrient cycle loop and promotes a circular economy.

Compost improves the fertility and structure of soil by providing plants with an abundance of nutrients. Compost's organic content increases microbial activity, aeration, and soil water retention. Additionally, compost functions as a slow-release fertilizer, giving plants easily accessible and absorbed forms of vital nutrients. Compost enhances soil tilth by acting as a soil conditioner, giving the soil a crumbly, well-organized texture. Consequently, this fosters robust root growth, improves resilience to soil erosion, and maintains a varied soil microbiome that is crucial for the general well-being of the soil.

Compost benefits soil carbon sequestration in addition to its role in soil fertility. Compost serves as a carbon reservoir due to its organic matter, and adding compost to the soil aids in the development and stabilization of soil organic carbon. This process improves soil resilience to extreme weather events, retains more water in the soil, and promotes long-term soil health, in addition to helping to mitigate the effects of climate change by sequestering carbon in the soil.

One crucial strategy for lowering greenhouse gas emissions is composting. Anaerobic landfill conditions, in which no oxygen is available for organic materials to break down, produce methane, a potent greenhouse gas. Methane emissions are significantly decreased by keeping organic waste out of landfills and encouraging aerobic decomposition in composting systems. This emphasizes the significance of sustainable waste management techniques and aligns with international efforts to slow down climate change.

Initiatives for community composting encourage involvement in the community and a sense of environmental responsibility. Community composting initiatives, whether started by grassroots groups, nonprofits, or local governments, give citizens easily accessible ways to get involved in trash reduction initiatives. Shared compost bins or community composting sites promote cooperation and education, uniting people behind the shared objective of sustainable waste management. These programs foster a sense of environmental stewardship in communities while lessening the adverse effects of organic waste on the ecosystem.

Recycling Strategies

A vital component of the effort to build a circular economy that is more sustainable is recycling. Recycling becomes an increasingly potent technique to alleviate resource depletion, decrease waste, and control the environmental impact of consumerism as the world grapples with mounting environmental concerns. This section explores the complex field of recycling strategies, looking at the various methods, difficulties, and new ideas that could revolutionize our thoughts on materials and waste.

Recycling is using old or abandoned materials to create new goods. The main objective is to replace the conventional linear economy with a closed-loop system in which resources are harvested, used, and dumped in landfills. Reusing, remanufacturing, and recycling materials is the foundation of the circular economy, which aims to reduce the environmental damage caused by resource extraction, production, and waste creation.

Municipal recycling is popular in which local governments set up mechanisms for gathering and sorting recyclable materials. Materials like paper, cardboard, glass, plastic, and metal are commonly included. Locals keep these products apart from other household rubbish, and special recycling centers sort, wash, and prepare them for remanufacturing. Municipal recycling programs must adhere to standardized norms and provide information to maximize their efficiency.

These programs differ significantly in terms of the materials accepted, the means of collection, and the processing capabilities.

One well-liked strategy in municipal recycling systems is single-stream recycling. This approach makes it easier for customers to sort their recyclables because they are all gathered into one bin. Single-stream recycling poses difficulties at the recycling plant even if it can increase participation and convenience. The quality and market value of recycled materials can be reduced by contamination, which occurs when non-recyclable materials or products that shouldn't be in the recycling stream are mixed in. Finding a balance between material purity and convenience is still a significant difficulty for municipal recycling systems.

A different approach to recycling is provided via deposit return schemes, mainly applicable to drink containers. Under this concept, customers buy beverage containers and pay a small deposit. The deposit is recovered when the empty container is returned to a designated collection station. Deposit return programs incentivize consumers to return containers with a monetary reward, promoting increased recycling rates. After being gathered, the containers are processed at recycling centers. Deposit return policies are beneficial in many areas, but their efficacy varies depending on the deposit amount, the simplicity of the return process, and customer knowledge.

The concept of extended producer responsibility (EPR) transfers the onus of recycling from end users to product makers. Producers are in charge of overseeing the recycling or end-of-life disposal of their products under an EPR framework. This tactic encourages producers to include easily recyclable materials in their designs, as well as to include take-back initiatives for old goods. Businesses are prompted to think about the environmental impact of their products from manufacture to disposal due to EPR, which promotes a more circular approach to product life cycles.

The recovery of materials and byproducts from manufacturing operations is the primary goal of industrial recycling. By recovering resources for reuse or remanufacturing, industrial recycling seeks to minimize the large amounts of waste that industries produce. The use of closed-loop systems, which involve the circulation of materials throughout the production process, can help enterprises reduce their environmental impact and the amount of fresh resources extracted. Industrial recycling promotes a more circular industrial economy by being consistent with sustainable production and resource efficiency.

Recycling of construction and demolition (C&D) trash deals with the significant waste produced in the construction sector. Much of the material used in building construction, renovation, and demolition can be recycled, including wood, metal, concrete, and asphalt. Recycling facilities for construction and demolition (C&D) sort and process these materials, keeping them out of landfills and using them in new construction projects. In addition to conserving resources, this method lessens the environmental effect of construction activities, promoting the creation of more sustainable and circular architecture and infrastructure.

The growing problem of electronic garbage, or e-waste, produced by abandoned electronic equipment is addressed by e-waste recycling. Electronic gadgets quickly become outdated due to the speed at which technology is developing, which causes an increase in e-waste. Recycling facilities for e-waste remove valuable materials from electronic equipment, including metals and plastics, preventing the environmental risks of incorrect disposal. In addition, the recycling of e-waste guarantees the secure and safe disposal of electronic components, lowering the possibility of dangerous materials polluting the environment.

One of the world's most significant sources of waste, the fashion industry, influences the environment, which is addressed through textile recycling. Fast fashion generates a lot of textile waste because of its quick production cycles and disposable apparel. By repurposing, reusing, or recycling textiles into new goods, textile recycling operations seek to increase the lifespan of textiles. Textile recycling innovations include chemical procedures that create new materials from discarded textile waste and mechanical processes that break down garments into fibers for reuse. Textile recycling reduces the environmental effect of textile production and disposal by encouraging circular practices in the fashion sector.

Compostable and biodegradable materials offer a viable way to lessen environmental impact. These products are meant to decompose organically via composting or microbiological processes. For example, biodegradable plastics are designed to break down naturally, minimizing the amount of plastic trash in the environment. Contrarily, materials that can be composted are meant to be placed in composting facilities, where they can decompose into organic matter. Although these materials have potential advantages, issues like appropriate disposal infrastructure, certification requirements, and consumer education must be resolved to guarantee their efficacy.

Technological advancements in recycling can completely transform the effectiveness and reach of recycling programs. Modern sorting technologies improve the accuracy and speed of material separation in recycling plants. Examples include robotics driven by artificial intelligence and optical sorting systems. Chemical recycling procedures aim to disassemble complicated polymers into their component monomers so that fresh plastic can be made without sacrificing quality. Innovations in upcycling encourage a change from linear to circular production processes by examining inventive ways to turn waste materials into higher-value goods.

Recycling tactics face difficulties, which calls for all-encompassing solutions and cooperative efforts. One major challenge that still affects the quality and marketability of recycled materials is contamination in recycling streams. Campaigns to educate and raise consumer knowledge about correct recycling and sorting techniques are essential in combating contamination. Furthermore, it is critical to improve infrastructure for product collecting and sorting, improve product design for recyclability, and promote industry collaboration.

Minimizing and Repurposing Waste

Reducing and reusing garbage has become essential to sustainable living in a world with rising environmental concerns and resource depletion. As people look for creative ways to lessen their ecological impact, the idea of a zero-waste lifestyle—which aims to send little or no garbage to landfills—has gained popularity. This section examines the various waste minimization and repurposing methods while looking at the transforming power of adopting a zero-waste attitude and its guiding principles.

Minimizing waste creation at its source is fundamental to waste minimization. Making decisions prioritizing avoiding single-use items, needless packaging, and disposable products is required. People who follow a zero-waste lifestyle frequently examine their consumption patterns, selecting products with long product lives, reusable alternatives, and minimum or recyclable packaging. Reducing the amount of unnecessary things that people bring into their lives can help people dramatically reduce the amount of waste they produce.

The circular economy philosophy emphasizes the value of extending the life of materials, which aligns with waste minimization. A closed-loop system where resources are reused, refurbished, remanufactured, and recycled is prioritized in a circular economy instead of following the linear extraction, manufacturing, consumption, and disposal model. This strategy necessitates a fundamental change in the conception, production, and consumption of goods. In a circular economy, extended product lifetimes, ease of repair, and disassembly are crucial factors promoting a more sustainable resource management method.

Upcycling and repurposing are inventive ways to keep things out of the trash and give them a new lease of life. Repurposing is showing objects that may otherwise be thrown away for further use. Commonplace household objects, like glass jars, can be used as decoration or storage, and with a bit of imagination, worn-out furniture can be made into something extraordinary. Repurposing is taken further with upcycling, turning waste materials into valuable goods. For example, wood pallets can be used to create chic furniture that enhances both appearance and functionality. Upcycling and repurposing promote a mentality change in which objects are seen as precious resources with unrealized potential rather than as waste.

The natural decomposition process of composting is an effective way to manage organic waste and turn it into soil rich in nutrients. People can keep much of their garbage out of landfills by composting yard waste, kitchen scraps, and other organic items. In addition to increasing soil fertility, compost also lowers the methane produced, a potent greenhouse gas produced during the anaerobic breakdown of organic matter. Composting systems are scalable solutions that turn organic waste into a valuable resource for gardening, landscaping, and agriculture. They can range in size from backyard bins to large-scale enterprises.

Recycling reduces waste before it is created by making conscientious decisions when purchasing. Precycling tactics center on cutting down on wasteful packaging, choosing products with sustainable or little packaging, and staying away from single-use items. Consumers may embrace precycling by purchasing goods in bulk, utilizing reusable containers, and patronizing companies that value minimum and environmentally friendly packaging. People can lessen the total environmental impact of consumerism by carefully contemplating the waste consequences of their choices.

Waste audits provide a systematic way to comprehend and deal with the types of waste produced in different contexts. Waste audits, which take place in residences, workplaces, or other establishments, entail separating and examining the many waste kinds generated. This procedure offers essential information about the percentage of organic trash, recyclables, and non-recyclables in the waste stream. With this data, people and institutions can customize their approaches to reducing waste, pinpoint opportunities for enhancement, and arrive at well-informed judgments regarding waste-handling procedures. Waste audits are a diagnostic tool that directs the creation of focused interventions to reduce waste production.

The idea behind "precious plastics" is to enable people and groups to address plastic pollution by setting up small-scale recycling plants. These open-source recycling machine ideas, created by the Precious Plastic initiative, allow plastic trash to be processed locally to create new items. Communities may use the Precious Plastic designs' readily available tools, such as shredders, extruders, injection, and compression molding machines, to transform plastic trash into valuable products. Precious plastics help reduce waste and provide a more circular approach to plastic use by decentralizing plastic recycling and supporting neighborhood efforts.

Using the maxim "reduce, reuse, recycle" as a compass aids resource conservation and waste management. The best way to prevent waste is to reduce consumption by selecting products with low environmental impact and considering whether purchases are necessary. Reusing

objects—whether by fixing, repurposing, or donating—
extends their life and keeps them out of the trash sooner.
The last phase in the motto, recycling, closes the circle of
the circular economy by processing materials to make new
goods. This three-pronged technique is a comprehensive
way for people to reduce their ecological impact on an
individual and community level.

The idea of a "circular supply chain" is becoming more
popular in the business world as organizations realize
how crucial it is to incorporate the ideas of the circular
economy into their daily operations. A circular supply
chain prioritizes the long-term viability and recyclability
of products while concentrating on the sustainable use
of resources. Businesses implementing circular supply
chain strategies develop their goods with end-of-life
sustainability in mind, making it easier to disassemble,
reuse, and recycle them. Adopting product-as-a-service
models, in which customers rent goods rather than buy
them, also promotes the transition to a circular
economy.

The ideas of resource efficiency and waste reduction. In
a closed-loop system, materials are recycled or put to
other uses when a product's life cycle is over, and it is
made to be readily disassembled. This method
contradicts the conventional linear model of production
and consumption, which calls for the disposal of
products once used. By encouraging a cyclical approach
where materials are continuously recycled and
repurposed, closed-loop production minimizes the
adverse effects of manufacturing on the environment
and lowers the need for new resources.

Waste-to-energy (WTE) technologies turn specific waste
kinds into electricity, offering an alternate method of
waste management. The techniques used in WTE
processes include anaerobic digestion, gasification, and
incineration. These technologies raise specific
environmental issues even if they can assist in

producing energy and minimize trash. Regulating emissions and disposing of ash and possibly hazardous byproducts are all important. WTE should be used with recycling and trash reduction rather than as a stand- alone remedy to provide a well-rounded and ecologically friendly waste management plan.

Initiatives that are rooted in the community are essential to attempts to reduce waste and reuse materials. These projects, which range from community composting programs to swap meets and repair cafes, encourage a sense of shared responsibility and give people the confidence to act as a group. Community-based initiatives provide a platform for exchanging goods, skills, and resources, promoting a more linked and sustainable approach to waste reduction. They also act as forums for awareness-raising, education, and developing a culture prioritizing environmental stewardship and resource conservation.

Technology integration provides creative ways to reduce waste and reuse materials. For example, mobile applications link people to nearby companies or groups that take and reuse particular products. Real-time data on garbage generation trends is provided via intelligent waste bins with sensors and data analytics, enabling more effective waste collection and management. In addition, new developments in material science and recycling technologies keep opening up new avenues for recycling a wider variety of materials, including textiles, plastics, and electronic waste.

The widespread culture of disposability, ingrained consumer behaviors, and a lack of infrastructure to support sustainable activities are obstacles to trash minimization and reuse techniques. Communities, corporations, governments, and individuals must work together to overcome these obstacles.

Adopting sustainable practices and modifying cultural norms are greatly aided by education and awareness efforts. Incentivizing firms can promote trash minimization by implementing circular economy ideas, enacting regulations that support trash reduction, and investing in recycling infrastructure.

Adopting a zero-waste mentality necessitates a comprehensive strategy encompassing personal decisions, neighborhood projects, commercial operations, and technology advancements. Repurposing and waste reduction are essential elements of a circular and sustainable economy, opposing the culture of disposability that is now in place and encouraging a more resource-aware lifestyle. The possibility of attaining a zero-waste future becomes a real and profound reality as people and society reassess their consumption habits, prioritize resource efficiency, and embrace novel approaches.

CHAPTER VIII

Off-Grid Technology

Off-Grid Communication Systems

As the world becomes more interconnected, communication is becoming necessary for day-to-day existence. Nonetheless, there are contexts and settings where conventional communication methods might not be feasible or easily accessible. Communication can be challenging in off-grid settings, isolated wilderness, disaster-affected areas, or even deliberate escapes from the grid. This section explores off-grid communication systems and the technologies and approaches that allow people to stay connected when traditional networks are unavailable.

The ability to create and sustain communication channels apart from centralized or conventional networks is known as "off-grid communication." This requirement emerges in various contexts, from outdoor activities and survival circumstances to deliberate off-grid living and emergency response operations. By bridging the connectivity gap, off-grid communication solutions enable people to collaborate, interact, and access information in isolated or remote locations.

A critical component of off-grid communication that is widely used is satellite communication, which provides worldwide coverage that is not limited by geographic location. Specifically, satellite phones enable data and voice connectivity in places without standard cellular networks. With the help of these phones, one may communicate from almost anywhere on Earth by connecting directly to satellites orbiting the planet. When faced with unforeseen difficulties in remote regions, satellite phones are handy as they enable people to contact for aid or coordinate rescue efforts. Furthermore, off-grid locations can now be connected to the internet using satellite internet services, facilitating communication, information retrieval, and disaster planning.

Radio transmission has provided a dependable and long-range means of communication in off-grid situations for many years. Two-way radios, sometimes called walkie-talkies, are commonly utilized for outdoor activities, events, and emergency response. They function on a variety of frequencies. Two-way radios are appropriate for off-grid communication as they don't depend on centralized infrastructure like cellular networks. Short- and long-range variants are available, and some are made specifically for outdoor activities like hiking, hunting, or boating. When going off the grid, emergency responders, outdoor enthusiasts, and isolated communities frequently rely on radio communication to stay in touch.

Mesh networks provide an adaptive and decentralized method for off-grid communication. Every device in a mesh network serves as a node, sending messages to other nodes in the network. This distributed architecture is exceptionally robust, allowing the network to adjust to topology changes or node loss. Mesh networks operate well in situations when traditional infrastructure is not accessible because they may make use of a variety of communication technologies, such as radio frequencies and Wi-Fi. When mesh networks are deployed in off-grid situations, communication channels can be created, which makes it easier for users to coordinate and share information.

In off-grid areas, drones carrying communication payloads are valuable instruments for creating transient communication linkages. Drones equipped with communication devices, like cellular repeaters or Wi-Fi hotspots, can establish connectivity temporarily in emergencies or distant areas. This skill is essential when it comes to search and rescue operations, disaster relief efforts, or circumstances where traditional communication infrastructure is disrupted. Responders can evaluate and handle urgent situations thanks to drones with communication relay capabilities, which increase the reach of communication networks.

Solar-powered and portable systems meet the off-grid communication demands of academics, outdoor enthusiasts, and people living in remote areas. A portable solar charger is a sustainable energy source for recharging communication devices like cell phones, radios, or satellite phones. Compact and lightweight satellite terminals are made for mobile use, guaranteeing that customers may maintain connectivity even when conventional power sources are unavailable. Because of their energy-efficient, weather-resistant, and durable construction, these off-grid communication devices are ideal for prolonged usage under challenging conditions.

A vital part of off-grid communication is played by amateur or ham radio enthusiasts, who offer a global network of operators capable of long-distance communication over specific frequencies. In times of crisis or tragedy, ham radio operators frequently assist with emergency communication by lending their equipment and expertise to support response operations. Amateur radio is a valuable tool in off-grid situations where traditional communication infrastructure can be unavailable or compromised because of its decentralized and self-sufficient character.

A state-of-the-art advancement in off-grid communication, Low Earth Orbit (LEO) satellite constellations offer improved worldwide coverage and lower latency. Prominent constellations of tiny satellites are being deployed in low Earth orbit by businesses like SpaceX's Starlink and OneWeb to provide broadband internet access in isolated and off-grid locations. By bridging the digital divide and providing high-speed internet connectivity, these satellite constellations enable individuals in remote areas to access online resources, communication, and information.

Off-grid communication is not just about technology; conventional messaging and signaling techniques are also essential. Low-tech communication techniques used for centuries include mirrors, smoke signals, flags, and Morse code. These methods are beneficial in situations where electrical gadgets might not be available or functional, such as outdoor survival scenarios. Acquiring knowledge and proficiency in these conventional communication techniques is advantageous for people traveling off the grid.

Strategies for communication off the grid are crucial to emergency response and readiness. Establishing alternative communication channels is essential for organizing rescue operations, sharing information, and expediting the delivery of supplies in disaster-stricken areas where traditional communication infrastructure may be destroyed or overburdened. In the wake of crises or natural catastrophes, rescuers can swiftly establish communication capabilities thanks to deployable communication technologies like portable satellite terminals and mobile cell-on-wheels (COW) units.

Communication systems are essential for keeping connected in isolated, self-sufficient communities when practicing purposeful off-grid living. To stay in touch with the outside world, plan events, and get vital information, residents of isolated research stations, off-grid cabins, and sustainable eco-villages depend on communication equipment. Off-grid communication systems for intentional communities frequently combine radio communication, satellite internet, and renewable energy sources to maintain continuous connectivity.

There are still issues with off-grid communication technology despite their progress. Obstacles in specific situations can include low satellite bandwidth, expensive equipment, and the requirement for a direct line of sight for satellite communication. The efficiency of off-grid communication networks may also be impacted by regulatory factors, spectrum allotment, and interoperability problems, particularly in cross-border or international scenarios. In keeping with sustainable and environmentally friendly methods, the environmental impact of installing and maintaining off-grid communication infrastructure must also be carefully considered.

Off-grid communication systems encompass a wide range of technologies and approaches intended to facilitate communication in situations when conventional networks are not available or not feasible. These systems meet off-grid requirements, ranging from satellite communication and mesh networks to mobile solar-powered options and traditional signaling techniques. The advancement of off-grid communication, whether in emergency response, outdoor activities, purposeful off-grid living, or remote research, empowers people and communities and promotes resilience and connectedness in the face of isolation.

Sustainable Internet and Connectivity

In a time where the digital revolution is king, having internet access has become essential to modern life. Our digital footprint's environmental and ethical ramifications are becoming increasingly apparent as the globe gets more connected. The notion of sustainable internet and connection aims to tackle the effects on the environment, energy usage, and moral issues related to the growth of digital infrastructure. To balance the development of technology and environmental responsibility, this section explores the obstacles, innovations, and prospective solutions surrounding the emerging field of sustainable internet activities.

Unquestionably, the spread of digital technologies and the widespread availability of internet connectivity have changed how we communicate, work, and live. The digital world has ingrained itself into our everyday lives, from cloud computing and streaming services to artificial intelligence and the Internet of Things (IoT). However, there is a price to this digital transformation: a sizable portion of the world's energy consumption and carbon emissions is attributed to the information and communication technology (ICT) sector.

In pursuing sustainable internet practices, data centers' energy consumption—the foundation of the digital infrastructure—must be considered. The servers that handle, store, and send enormous volumes of digital data are housed in data centers. The energy consumption of these facilities has increased due to their energy-intensive nature and the growing need for processing and data storage capacity. To reduce the environmental impact of data center operations, sustainable data center initiatives prioritize energy efficiency optimization, using renewable energy sources, and using cutting-edge cooling technology.

Integrating renewable energy is an essential tactic in the quest for sustainable internet activities. Numerous multinational corporations and operators of data centers have pledged to shift their operations to rely exclusively on renewable energy sources. Data centers use electricity produced by solar and wind power, which minimizes the carbon footprint associated with digital infrastructure and lessens dependency on fossil fuels. PPAs and on-site renewable energy installations are two ways the ICT industry goes green, encouraging a more ecologically conscious and sustainable approach to internet connectivity.

With the potential for sustainability advantages, the move toward edge computing offers a fundamental evolution in the data processing. By processing data nearer to the point of generation, edge computing minimizes the need for centralized data centers and the energy needed for long-distance data transmission. Edge computing provides lower latency solutions and increases efficiency by sharing processing resources among a network of edge devices, such as Internet of Things devices or local servers. This decentralized method minimizes the environmental impact of data processing while improving resource consumption, which is consistent with sustainability ideals.

Technological advancements in cooling are essential for improving data center energy efficiency. Conventional cooling techniques for data centers, including air conditioning, consume much energy and raise overall operating expenses. Sustainable cooling solutions aim to use less energy to maintain the ideal temperatures for server operation. These solutions include liquid cooling, natural ventilation, and innovative cooling architectures. These developments lessen the environmental impact and improve the general energy efficiency of data center operations.

In the ICT industry, the circular economy idea is becoming increasingly popular. It emphasizes the ethical handling of electronic trash, or "e-waste," produced by outdated or discarded gadgets. Recycling procedures can be used to recover valuable resources from e-waste, such as rare earth elements and precious metals. Designing devices with modularity and simplicity of disassembly facilitates component recovery and reuse, a component of sustainable practices. Additionally, safe handling and disposal of hazardous materials is ensured by responsible e-waste management, reducing the danger of environmental degradation and health hazards that come with inappropriate e-waste disposal.

Building a genuinely sustainable digital environment requires ethical concerns in addition to energy efficiency and waste management in creating and implementing sustainable Internet practices. Concerns like digital inclusion, privacy, and the responsible use of developing technology are among the ethical aspects of internet access. Ensuring universal access to the internet's benefits or bridging the digital divide is an essential moral requirement. Initiatives are concentrated on offering inexpensive and easily accessible internet connectivity to marginalized populations to promote digital inclusion and solve social inequities.

Privacy issues have spurred debates about user rights and moral data practices in the digital age. Informed permission, transparent data handling, and robust cybersecurity safeguards to preserve user privacy are all components of sustainable Internet practices. Ethical considerations must be made while using data analytics, artificial intelligence, and machine learning to avoid prejudice, discrimination, and the improper use of personal data. By prioritizing ethical data practices, the ICT sector can foster user trust and lessen the possible harmful effects of technology on people and society.

The creation and application of developing technologies are also subject to the incorporation of ethical considerations. Consider the potential and problems that artificial intelligence brings to the pursuit of ethical and sustainable online behavior. Fairness, accountability, transparency, and inclusivity are all part of the moral AI tenets. To develop AI responsibly, it is necessary to eliminate algorithmic biases, guarantee accountability for AI judgments, and encourage transparency in AI systems. The information and communications technology industry may help build a sustainable digital future that benefits society by coordinating AI development with ethical issues.

International cooperation and projects greatly aid the global advancement of sustainable Internet practices. For instance, governments, businesses, and civil society organizations come together under the Paris Call for Trust and Security in Cyberspace to advance a shared vision for guaranteeing cyberspace's safety and moral use. The mission of the Alliance for Affordable Internet (A4AI) is to promote legislative and regulatory changes that will lower the cost and increase global access to Internet services. Initiatives like this highlight how interconnected the digital world is and how we must work together to solve the moral and environmental issues raised by internet connectivity.

The idea of "tech for good" highlights how technology may help address environmental and social issues. Sustainable internet practices encourage the ethical application of technology to solve global concerns, consistent with the ideas of tech for good. Events like the Tech for Good Global Summit bring together advocates, legislators, and entrepreneurs to discuss how technology may help achieve sustainable development objectives. The information and communications technology (ICT) sector may effect good change and help create a more just and sustainable world by utilizing technology for social and environmental benefits.

Adopting sustainable internet practices poses several challenges, such as the requirement for international norms and laws, technology breakthroughs, and industry cooperation. Encouraging a culture of ethical considerations in technical innovation, guaranteeing the accessibility of sustainable technologies in various places, and creating widely recognized methods for quantifying the environmental impact of digital infrastructure are all ongoing issues. But these difficulties also offer chances for cooperation, creativity, and the group's joint quest for a responsible and sustainable digital future.

Smart Technologies for Off-Grid Living

The appeal of living off the grid, characterized by self-reliance and a close relationship with the natural world, has been embraced by an expanding group of people who want to live more sustainably and lessen their influence on the environment. The off-grid experience has been completely transformed in recent years by incorporating innovative technology, which provides creative ways to improve comfort, efficiency, and environmental stewardship. This section examines the range of innovative technology available for off-grid living, examining the various uses that enable people to live in balance with the environment and reap the rewards of contemporary innovation.

The main obstacle to off-grid life is obtaining electricity independently, frequently from renewable sources. Optimizing energy generation, storage, and consumption in off-grid environments is primarily made possible by intelligent energy management systems. These systems use sophisticated algorithms and real-time data analytics to balance the energy production from solar panels, wind turbines, or other renewable sources with the demand from various appliances and gadgets. Intelligent energy management systems increase efficiency, extend the life of energy storage devices, and support a more sustainable off-grid energy infrastructure by cleverly managing energy flows.

With the development of intelligent solar technology, solar energy—a vital component of off-grid power—has undergone a revolutionary change. With sensors and embedded intelligence, bright solar panels can automatically change their tilt and orientation to maximize the sunshine they absorb throughout the day. These panels also can interface with energy storage systems and inverters, allowing for real-time modifications in response to changes in the weather and energy consumption. Innovative solar technology increases solar efficiency and adaptability, strengthening and increasing the dependability of the off-grid energy environment.

An essential component of off-grid life is energy storage, which offers a consistent power source when renewable energy production isn't as high. Thanks to intelligent battery management systems, advanced lead-acid and lithium-ion batteries are two examples of energy storage options with improved performance and endurance. These systems use predictive algorithms to optimize the charging and discharging cycles, avoiding overcharging or deep draining, which can jeopardize the battery's health. Integrating intelligent energy storage technologies guarantees a steady and reliable power supply even without instantaneous renewable energy generation.

Smart home automation is one of the mainstays of integrating technology with off-grid life. Smart home automation systems improve Energy efficiency and convenience which may control thermostats, lights, and appliances. Real-time monitoring and control of several home operations are made possible by sensors and actuators, allowing inhabitants to customize their living space and maximize energy efficiency. Smart home automation offers off-grid homeowners a smooth transition between sustainability and contemporary comfort, promoting an eco-friendly and cutting-edge way of living.

Water management is crucial when living off the grid because getting a steady water supply might take a lot of work. Off-grid homeowners may optimize water usage, identify leaks, and guarantee the sustainability of their water sources with the help of intelligent water monitoring and conservation systems. IoT-based sensors can track storage tank water levels, examine usage trends, and notify users of possible problems. When combined with weather forecasting algorithms, intelligent irrigation systems allow for exact watering schedules that save water waste and enhance crop productivity in off-grid gardens and agricultural endeavors.

Off-grid living environments become more intelligent and connected with the addition of Internet of Things (IoT) devices. Monitoring resource use, security, and environmental conditions with intelligent sensors and actuators is possible. For instance, sensors for temperature and humidity help regulate the environment, and sensors for motion improve security by setting off alarms when they detect unusual behavior. Connecting these Internet of Things gadgets to a smart home hub allows you to automate and centrally regulate several tasks, making your off-grid living space more flexible and responsive.

With the introduction of intelligent connectivity options, off-grid communications have undergone a technical revolution. Reliable communication in remote and off-grid regions is possible via satellite communication, mesh networks, and long-range radio technology. Off-grid inhabitants can stay in touch with the outside world, obtain information, and plan activities with the help of portable, user-friendly smart satellite terminals. By bridging the connectivity gap, these communication solutions enable off-grid communities, travelers, and academics to ensure that isolation does not mean disconnection.

With the help of intelligent technologies, precision agriculture is revolutionizing off-grid farming and sustainable food production. Innovative farming methods maximize crop management, irrigation, and pest control by utilizing data from sensors, drones, and weather stations. Off-grid farmers can reduce their environmental impact, maximize harvests, and conserve resources using precision agriculture. Using GPS and sensor data to guide automated agricultural equipment enhances the sustainability and effectiveness of off-grid agriculture, facilitating a peaceful cohabitation with the environment.

Waste management assumes a clever dimension when living off the grid because conserving resources is crucial. Innovative waste monitoring systems can optimize waste collection routes and schedules by using sensors to monitor garbage bin fill levels. These methods lessen the need for needless transportation, use less fuel, and help to manage waste more effectively. Furthermore, intelligent composting systems use IoT technology to monitor and regulate composting conditions, guaranteeing that organic waste breaks down quickly and produces rich compost that can be used in off-grid gardens and agricultural practices.

Water self-sufficiency and off-grid living go hand in hand, and intelligent technologies are essential to conserving and maximizing water use. Innovative filtration and purification devices make off-grid water sources safe and high-quality. Real-time water quality monitoring is possible with IoT-enabled sensors, giving locals knowledge about the condition of their water source. By scheduling their operations to occur during periods of maximum energy output, smart water heaters, and pumps can reduce the amount of energy needed for water-related tasks. These developments provide an all-encompassing strategy for managing water in off-grid settings.

Blockchain technology's decentralized and secure characteristics make it useful in off-grid living situations, especially when managing renewable energy resources. Peer-to-peer energy trading platforms, built on blockchain technology, allow off-grid communities to buy and sell excess energy among themselves. This decentralized strategy promotes a community-driven energy ecology by doing away with intermediaries. Furthermore, blockchain-based systems encourage moral and environmentally friendly resource acquisition methods by improving the traceability and transparency of off-grid supply chains.

Off-grid technology integration with artificial intelligence (AI) gives up new possibilities for productivity and flexibility. Artificial intelligence (AI) algorithms can evaluate past energy usage patterns, weather forecasts, and user preferences to enhance the performance of off-grid energy systems. Off-grid systems can be more predictive by applying machine learning techniques, enabling them to foresee changes in weather, energy consumption, and equipment maintenance requirements. As a result, off-grid living has become more clever, robust, and convenient.

The adoption of innovative technology for off-grid living is hampered by upfront costs, the requirement for dependable connectivity, and technological proficiency. Some off-grid people may need help to make the upfront investments in smart devices and systems, especially if they have a limited budget. In addition, for people to successfully integrate innovative technology into off-grid lifestyles, it is critical to guarantee that they possess the knowledge and abilities needed to operate and maintain these devices. In distant and off-grid places, reliable connectivity—via satellite communication or another method—is essential to the smooth operation of intelligent technology.

In summary, off-grid living is changing due to intelligent technology, which provides a seamless fusion of contemporary and sustainability. Precision farming, water conservation, energy management, and home automation are just a few technologies that enable off-grid dwellers to live independent, green lives. The potential for improving off-grid living's sustainability, comfort, and efficiency is growing as smart technology integration continues to develop. Through adopting these advancements, people and communities can usher in a new phase of off-grid living.

CHAPTER IX

Achieving Financial Independence

Budgeting for Off-Grid Living

Living off the grid signifies a significant change toward sustainability and self-sufficiency. Off-grid life has many advantages, such as no utility costs, less of an impact on the environment, and a stronger bond with the natural world. Still, it also necessitates careful budgeting and financial planning. The complexities of budgeting for off-grid life are examined in this section, along with essential factors, possible roadblocks, and workable solutions to guarantee financial stability while pursuing self-sufficiency.

Budgeting for off-grid living is around determining how much money is needed for necessities such as energy, water, food, shelter, and infrastructure. Off-grid enthusiasts frequently invest in renewable energy sources like solar or wind turbines to meet their electrical needs. These systems save money over time by doing away with monthly utility payments, even though the initial investment can be high. Estimating the expenses of installation, upkeep, and any backup power systems required is part of budgeting for renewable energy, which guarantees a dependable and sustainable energy source for off-grid living.

A key component of off-grid life is water self-sufficiency, necessitating careful planning for water harvesting, storage, and purification systems. Rainwater collection, wells, and other sustainable water sources must be evaluated regarding their upfront costs, continuing upkeep, and possible infrastructure needs. Systems for purifying water, like UV sterilizers or filters, must also be considered. One of the primary requirements of off-grid life is a steady and secure supply of water, which may be ensured through effective budgeting.

Off-grid aficionados frequently opt for alternate housing alternatives like tiny homes, cabins, or earthships for shelter. Off-grid house budgeting entails assessing labor and material expenses and incorporating ecological and energy-efficient design ideas. Off-grid residents can also consider the costs of obtaining permissions, purchasing land, and building infrastructure. Finding a balance between affordability and the long-term viability and comfort of the selected shelter is a crucial part of the budgeting process.

A thoughtful approach to food production and storage is required for off-grid life, which affects the budget and overall level of self-sufficiency. Budgetary concerns encompass the creation of gardens, greenhouses, aquaponics systems, and the acquisition of seeds, soil, and implements. Living off the grid also allows people to budget for chickens and cattle, which supports a sustainable approach to food production. Setting up money for long-term food storage options, including root cellars or equipment for food preservation, guarantees a steady and dependable source of food all year round.

Off-grid budgeting heavily relies on infrastructure investments, which include waste management, communication networks, and road access. Building a sturdy and dependable infrastructure is critical to off-grid living's sustainability and functionality. Budgetary considerations encompass the expenses associated with building roads, disposing of waste, and implementing communication technology that enables connectivity in isolated areas. Infrastructure should be strategically budgeted to guarantee that off-grid dwellers have the building blocks for robust and independent living.

Off-grid living can result in lower monthly costs but also necessitates an initial investment in necessary infrastructure and technologies. Planning for future improvements or expansions, comprehending the continuing maintenance needs, and evaluating these upfront expenditures are crucial for a thorough budget. A well-defined and pragmatic budget is a financial decision-making guide, empowering off-grid enthusiasts to distribute resources effectively and avoid unforeseen financial obstacles while pursuing self-sufficiency.

Off-grid life requires being prepared for emergencies,

and creating a contingency budget guarantees financial stability in the face of unforeseen difficulties. Residents living off the grid might save money for emergency communication equipment, medical supplies, or backup power systems. Budgeting for an emergency fund strengthens the off-grid lifestyle's overall stability by providing a financial buffer for unforeseen costs. When external support systems are not readily available, having a well-prepared budget becomes essential to preserving financial stability in times of need.

Off-grid living revolves around thrift and

resourcefulness, which impact financial choices at every stage. Off-grid fans frequently lead a simple lifestyle, putting necessities ahead of extravagance. Budgeting for off-grid living entails deliberate decision-making and creating a distinction between needs and wants. By developing a thrifty mindset, people and communities can reduce waste, maximize their budget, and improve the sustainability of their off-grid lifestyle.

Off-grid life in a community brings new factors to

account for when creating a budget. Off-grid people's financial obligations may change due to pooled resources, cooperative projects, and shared infrastructure. In a communal context, budgeting calls for open communication, reaching a consensus, and a shared understanding of financial obligations. Collective efforts, such as shared water systems, bulk buying, or communal gardening, can save costs and increase the off-grid group's overall economic resilience.

A key component of off-grid living budgeting is assessing return on investment (ROI), which directs financial decisions based on long-term advantages. Even though some off-grid infrastructure and technologies may cost more upfront, estimating the possible savings over time is crucial. For example, although solar panels may require a more considerable initial investment, they can result in significant long-term savings by doing away with or significantly lowering monthly electricity expenses. Off-grid enthusiasts should use an ROI- focused budget to pick the investments that yield the most sustainable and economical returns.

Acquiring knowledge and skills is a crucial aspect of off-grid living, impacting financial considerations and lifestyle selections. Developing fundamental abilities like gardening, carpentry, or maintaining renewable energy sources enables off-grid dwellers to lessen their need for outside assistance and cut expenses. Setting aside money for continuing education, workshops, or training courses helps those interested in living off the grid become more resilient and self-sufficient.

Technology-enhanced budgeting procedures improve the effectiveness and transparency of off-grid financial management. For off-grid fans, digital tools like spreadsheet software and budgeting apps make it easy to manage expenditures, create financial goals, and examine spending trends. Effective financial management guarantees that budgeting stays flexible and dynamic, enabling people and communities to make well-informed choices and adaptations while navigating the opportunities and difficulties associated with living off the grid.

Budgeting for off-grid life can be tricky because of the possibility of underestimating start-up costs, unforeseen maintenance expenditures, and income changes. To meet these obstacles, in-depth investigation, practical evaluations, and backup plans are critical. Furthermore, flexibility and frequent reevaluation are necessary to adjust the budget to changing conditions, such as modifications in energy usage or changing community demands.

In summary, creating an off-grid budget is a complex and dynamic process that requires careful consideration of several variables. Off-grid budgeting entails strategically deploying resources to support a sustainable and self-sufficient living, ranging from energy and water systems to housing, food production, and emergency preparedness. The full potential of an off-grid lifestyle that promotes harmony with nature and a minor environmental impact can be unlocked by individuals and groups navigating the financial hurdles of off-grid living by developing economic resilience, embracing frugality, and utilizing technology.

Income-Generating Strategies

Living off the grid is a way to pursue sustainability, self-sufficiency, and a closer relationship with the natural world. Off-grid life has many advantages, but financial considerations need to be carefully considered. Off-grid fans frequently look for ways to generate cash and budget for necessities to sustain their distinctive way of life. To achieve financial independence while enjoying the peace of self-sufficient living, this section addresses a variety of income-generating strategies designed for off-grid life.

Adopting homesteading and sustainable agriculture is one of the main ways that off-grid living generates cash. Off-grid residents can grow a wide range of fruits, vegetables, and crops to meet their nutritional needs and to make money by selling extra goods to nearby markets or through community-supported agriculture (CSA) initiatives. Furthermore, off-grid farms become more resilient when using permaculture, agroforestry, or organic farming methods. This gives environmentally aware consumers a way to support sustainable agriculture.

Managing livestock and poultry offers an additional source of income for those living off the grid. Eggs, milk, honey, and meat for sale or personal use can be produced by raising animals like hens, goats, or bees. Off-grid enthusiasts exploit the growing desire for locally sourced and sustainably grown food by exploring niche markets for organic or ethically produced animal goods. The combination of holistic management and rotational grazing techniques enhances the ecological equilibrium of off-grid farms.

In an off-grid setting, cottage businesses and artisanal crafts flourish, providing residents with a creative outlet and possible sources of income. Developing talents like woodworking, ceramics, soap making, candle making, or textile arts into small-scale enterprises is likely. Handmade goods can be sold in local markets, craft fairs, or internet marketplaces, giving off-grid artisans a way to reach a broader customer base and vary their sources of revenue. These goods' distinctive, handmade quality frequently appeals to those looking for natural, sustainable substitutes.

Online entrepreneurship and remote employment have emerged as practical means of producing revenue for people living off the grid in the digital age. People can use their skills and knowledge regardless of where they live by freelancing, consulting, or operating an internet business. Reliable internet connectivity makes virtual cooperation possible, even in rural regions. This allows off-grid enthusiasts to offer writing, graphic design, programming, and digital marketing services. Online and e-commerce platforms provide a worldwide market for goods made in the peace of off-grid environments. Cooperative income-generating endeavors can strengthen financial resilience, and off-grid living frequently promotes a strong feeling of community. Collective endeavors, like communal gardens, shared artisan workshops, or cooperative farming, allow off-grid dwellers to combine resources and labor. In addition to sharing the effort, community-supported projects provide doors for group marketing and sales, strengthening the off-grid community's overall financial stability.

Ecotourism and instructional programs capitalize on the natural beauty and sustainable practices of the environment to provide off-grid lifestyle enthusiasts with unique chances to earn revenue. Off-grid homeowners might give seminars, retreats, or narrated tours highlighting their lifestyle, eco-friendly habits, and the local environment. Off-grid hosts might receive additional revenue from guests who pay for lodging, workshops, or guided excursions to provide them with a genuine off-grid experience. Programs that teach permaculture, sustainable living, or renewable energy might also draw students who want to learn about and gain skills related to living off the grid.

Off-grid living frequently entails a dedication to environmental care, and this mindset can extend to producing revenue through environmentally responsible endeavors. Off-grid living concepts are supported by starting a native plant nursery, heirloom seed propagation, or sustainable design-focused landscaping services. Similarly, eco-consulting services that steer companies or people toward more sustainable practices can support the preservation of the environment and sound financial management.

For those living off the grid, incorporating renewable energy sources presents opportunities for revenue generation and energy independence. In some places, net metering systems allow surplus energy from solar or wind turbines to be sold back to the grid. Off-grid residents might look into options to start their energy businesses by joining community energy cooperatives or selling sustainable energy to nearby towns. This multipurpose application of renewable energy technologies supports the off-grid lifestyle's financial viability and the more significant shift to clean, decentralized energy.

Living off the grid frequently entails a close relationship with nature, and this relationship can spark creative pursuits that generate revenue. Off-grid writers, photographers, singers, and artists may find inspiration in their location to produce works that appeal to people concerned about the environment and the natural world. Off-grid creatives can share their viewpoints and profit from their interest by selling artwork, literature, or music through internet stores, neighborhood markets, or galleries.

Off-grid landowners can use investing in ecotourism or hospitality businesses, like creating eco-friendly cabins or campgrounds, to produce income. In addition to offering financial benefits, a retreat to nature enthusiasts, environmentally concerned tourists, or anyone looking for a vacation from the city allows you to showcase the serenity and beauty of off-grid living to a larger audience. Promoting responsible tourism practices, guided natural experiences, and sustainable lodging all add to the allure of off-grid hospitality.

Living off the grid promotes ingenuity, which includes considering upcycling and repurposing materials as possible sources of income. Reclaimed wood, salvaged materials, or abandoned objects can be turned into useful objects with a distinctive history that can be used as furniture or décor. Off-grid artists who inventively repurpose materials have a market because of the growing appeal of sustainable and repurposed products, which promotes both environmental preservation and economic sustainability.

While there are many opportunities for off-grid living income-generating tactics, there are obstacles to overcome in terms of market accessibility, legal constraints, and the seasonality of some businesses.

Off-grid business owners must perform an in-depth study and communicate with local authorities because zoning restrictions, licensing requirements, and compliance with local laws can differ. Accessing markets can provide logistical difficulties, especially for isolated off-grid areas, which may require innovative marketing and distribution strategies. Furthermore, because some sources of income are seasonal—like agriculture—off- grid dwellers might need to plan for different revenue sources at varying times of the year.

In summary, income-generating off-grid living techniques enable people and groups to embrace a self-sufficient and sustainable way of life while achieving financial freedom. Depending on their abilities, hobbies, and surroundings, off-grid dwellers can choose to pursue online entrepreneurship from various opportunities, such as ecotourism, artisanal crafts, and sustainable agriculture. Off-grid enthusiasts may unlock the full potential of financial freedom in the tranquility of self-sufficient living by embracing innovation, teamwork, and a commitment to environmental stewardship as they negotiate the chances and obstacles of income generating.

Barter and Trade in Off-Grid Communities

The core values of off-grid living include sustainability, independence, and a sense of belonging to one's local community. Old-fashioned commerce and barter have come back into favor in off-grid communities as a way to facilitate exchanges that support the values of resourcefulness and self-sufficiency. This section explores the dynamics of barter and trade in off-grid communities, examining the reasons behind, advantages of, and difficulties associated with these long-standing economic practices essential to developing an independent and resilient off-grid way of life.

Bartering, or direct exchange of products and services without money, has a long history that predates the creation of the contemporary monetary system. Barter arises in off-grid communities as a logical and natural solution to the problems with conventional currency-based interactions. Economic transactions are decentralized, which fits well with the off-grid lifestyle's self-sufficiency philosophy. Residents can use their excess resources and abilities in a system that values sustainability and mutual gain.

The physical bond that barter creates between members of off-grid communities is one of the main reasons it is so common. Barter adds a human element to economic trade in a world where computerized transactions and impersonal exchanges are becoming increasingly prevalent. In-person negotiations, people in off-grid villages develop relationships and a sense of trust beyond the transaction. In addition to strengthening ties within the community, this interpersonal relationship guarantees a more flexible and resilient economic system.

Resource use and talent sharing are crucial to barter and commerce in off-grid societies. Locals are skilled in various trades, from carpentry and farming to artisanal crafts and renewable energy. Through bartering, people can make their abilities available to the community, fostering an environment where each person contributes by their areas of strength. This cooperative strategy increases the community's overall level of self-sufficiency and promotes the ongoing acquisition and sharing of valuable skills necessary for off-grid living.

In off-grid settlements, the use of swap helps lessen the environmental impact. In off-grid communities, barter promotes a circular economy in a society where the linear model of production and consumption is dominant. Reusing, recycling, and repurposing goods increases their lifespan and reduces waste. This environmentally friendly strategy embodies a dedication to responsible resource management and is consistent with the off-grid lifestyle's innate environmental conscience.

Off-grid communities benefit from the absence of traditional cash in barter transactions, which reduces the impact of outside economic influences. In traditional economies, changes in the value of currencies, inflation, and economic downturns can all domino effect on people's purchasing power. By acting as a buffer against these vulnerabilities, barter enables those living off the grid to preserve a more stable economic environment free from the volatility of the world's financial institutions. One of the main components of the independent way of life that people who are adopting off-grid living seek is financial independence.

In off-grid communities, barter is a tool for constructing social capital and exchanging commodities and services. Barter transactions foster a sense of community interdependence by promoting cooperation and communication due to their informal nature. Successful bartering relationships are based on trust and reciprocity, creating a sense of community where people are driven by the welfare of the group and their own interests. This interconnectedness fuels off-grid communities' adaptation and resilience.

In off-grid settlements, various resources and talents foster a vibrant barter economy. Communities that depend on agriculture might exchange fresh produce for carpentry services, and people knowledgeable about renewable energy sources could trade their talents for handcrafted goods. This diversity fosters a culture of appreciation for each member's many skills and contributions while also ensuring a well-rounded and self-sufficient community. In this setting, barter transforms into a celebration of the richness that results from the community's combined resources and abilities.

Off-grid communities can benefit significantly from swap, but there are also drawbacks. The complexity of negotiations may arise from the absence of a standard unit of value. In contrast to money transactions, which rely on objective evaluations of worth, barter depends on subjective assessments of the worth of products and services. Effective communication, trust, and a shared understanding of the value placed on various goods and services within the community are necessary for negotiating fair and equitable transactions.

The seasonality of some supplies and talents also affects barter exchanges in off-grid communities. For example, the seasons affect how readily available fresh produce is in agricultural towns. This seasonality might affect the trade balance and call for adaptable and flexible bartering strategies. To maintain a constant and mutually beneficial flow of products and services, residents must be aware of the natural rhythms of their surroundings and modify their trading activities accordingly.

Traditional barter in off-grid villages has taken on new dimensions due to technological advancements. Although bartering is fundamentally based on face-to-face exchanges, digital networks, and internet platforms have arisen to make transactions easier. Off-grid residents can advertise their needs, wants, and services on social media groups or community-based websites, which broadens the barter market beyond their close neighbors. To guarantee that technology enhances rather than diminishes the interpersonal and social aspects of traditional bartering, off-grid societies must exercise caution when incorporating technology into their trade practices.

To improve the effectiveness of barter in off-grid communities, open lines of communication and transparent procedures are necessary. Establishing community standards, norms, and expectations around barter exchanges promotes a fair and cooperative atmosphere. Frequent community meetings offer a forum to discuss needs, resources, and possible joint ventures. These meetings also help to foster relationships and efficient communication. Having clear communication also makes it easier to resolve any disputes or miscommunications that can occur during the bartering process.

In off-grid communities, barter refers to more than just exchanging material products and services—it also includes exchanging information and life lessons. Events such as workshops, skill-sharing sessions, and group learning become essential for the barter system. Along with exchanging tangible goods, locals often share knowledge, perspectives, and valuable skills supporting the community's resilience and overall development.

In off-grid communities, barter and trade provide a traditional and flexible economic model that fits with sustainability, self-sufficiency, and communal cohesion. Beyond the simple trade of goods for services, barter strengthens social ties, creates social capital, and increases the economic and environmental robustness of off-grid living. Although there are difficulties, barter's advantages—which include a minor ecological impact and the strengthening of social ties—underline its continued significance in the setting of off-grid communities, where a spirit of self-reliance and cooperation is encouraged.

CHAPTER X

Overcoming Common Challenges

Social Isolation

Social isolation contradicts modern life in an era of unparalleled connectedness. People worldwide struggle with isolation and disconnection despite the widespread use of social media and digital communication. This section explores the many facets of social isolation, including its causes, symptoms, and detrimental effects on relationships, mental health, and community cohesion. In an increasingly interconnected world, it is critical to comprehend the causes and effects of social isolation to promote a culture that places a high value on genuine connection and wellbeing.

Physical separation is only one aspect of the complicated and subtle phenomena of social isolation. It includes the subjective experience of feeling cut off from critical social contacts even when surrounded by others or participating in virtual groups. While social isolation can also result from physical isolation, such as living in a remote area, it can also occur in highly populated urban areas, places of employment, or even among families that appear to be close. Social isolation has taken on a new dimension in the digital age, when people may, ironically, feel alone in a sea of virtual contacts.

Many variables contribute to social isolation, including personal, societal, and technological aspects. Face-to-face contact is declining due to modern lifestyles characterized by busy schedules, long workdays, and a predominance of screen-based interactions. While remote work offers freedom, it may unintentionally result in fewer opportunities for socializing in regular professional environments. In addition, cultural transformations, societal norms, and personal preferences all significantly impact how social dynamics are shaped and how connected or isolated people feel.

In the context of social isolation, technological advancements—especially the widespread use of social media—present a dilemma. Although these platforms are supposed to help people interact with one another across distances, they also make people feel disconnected. Inadequacy and isolation can be exacerbated by carefully constructed online personas, comparison-driven content, and the possibility of cyberbullying. Ironically, the digital era—meant to improve communication—has contributed to social isolation and loneliness.

The long-term effects of social isolation outweigh any transient loneliness. Long-term social isolation is becoming more widely acknowledged as a significant risk factor for mental health problems. Extended periods of social isolation are frequently associated with depression, anxiety, and elevated stress levels. People who don't have robust social support systems are more susceptible to the negative impacts of stress, which makes them less resilient to life's obstacles. Furthermore, as irregular social interaction can affect mental health and brain function, social isolation has been connected to cognitive decline.

Social isolation affects people at all phases of life, influencing not just the individual but also relationships and communities. Extended periods of isolation can hinder the development of social skills, self-esteem, and a sense of identity during adolescence, a crucial time for social growth. As they navigate the challenges of relationships and careers, young adults may experience feelings of loneliness as they struggle with conformity pressure and cultural expectations. Social isolation is a common worry among the senior population, which is frequently made worse by conditions including declining physical health, losing friends or family, and moving to a different residence.

Social isolation hurts relationships, whether they are romantic or platonic. Partners in intimate relationships may struggle with emotions of loneliness on their own, which can lead to a lack of emotional connection. When people withdraw from social circles, friendships may erode, affecting shared experiences and a sense of community. Social isolation can lead to a vicious cycle in which the breakdown of relationships fuels further isolation, undermining the foundation of social ties.

As groups, communities encounter difficulties when social isolation spreads among their constituents. Mutual support, a network of relationships, and shared experiences are the foundation of a sense of community. Social ties deteriorate when people stop taking part in communal activities. This loss of social capital impacts communities' resilience, cohesiveness, and general well-being. The strength of individual relationships within a community determines its overall health in an interconnected world.

A multimodal strategy that considers human, societal, and technological aspects is needed to address social isolation. A key component of societal interventions is fostering a culture that appreciates and emphasizes social ties. Policies that support social inclusion, community involvement, and work-life balance help create a social structure that lessens social isolation. Campaigns for education and awareness can question social norms that support solitude and emphasize the value of mental health and wellbeing.

The critical component of technological interventions is reevaluating digital platforms' contribution to developing meaningful connections. Although social media can facilitate connections, it takes a team effort to overcome its bad parts. The digital landscape can be changed by promoting online environments that value genuine connections, pleasant interactions, and encouraging communities. Technology businesses have a part to play in creating platforms that contribute to fundamental social interactions rather than take away from them.

Emergency Preparedness

Being prepared for emergencies is crucial in a world of uncertainty and unforeseen difficulties. People and communities confront a variety of potential emergencies, ranging from natural disasters to health crises and unanticipated events, necessitating a proactive and planned approach to preparedness. This section examines the essential components of emergency preparedness and the value of individual accountability, community involvement, and planning in reducing uncertainty and enhancing resilience in the face of unforeseen events.

Fundamentally, disaster preparedness is an all-encompassing, forward-thinking approach meant to reduce the effects of unanticipated events and guarantee quick and efficient response systems. Emergencies cover many situations, including artificial crises like industrial accidents, pandemics, and other unforeseen catastrophes, as well as natural disasters like hurricanes, earthquakes, and floods. The aim of creating an emergency preparation plan is to respond to crises as they arise and lessen their effects by taking preventative actions that increase resilience in general.

The foundation of any successful emergency preparedness is planning. A well-defined emergency plan that is updated regularly can benefit individuals, families, and communities by outlining precise steps to take before, during, and after a disaster. Evacuation routes, communication plans, emergency contacts, and necessary supplies are all part of a comprehensive strategy. Planning also includes identifying regional vulnerabilities and local dangers to guarantee that disaster preparedness measures are customized to particular risks and situations.

Participation in the community is essential to emergency preparedness since a community's strength as a whole dramatically increases its ability to endure and recover from crises. Neighborhood groups, local government organizations, and community-based organizations are all important in promoting a preparedness culture. Working together, community members and stakeholders can guarantee thorough emergency planning, efficient resource allocation, and strong communication lines. Community drills and simulations also help people become more aware and prepared, which makes it possible for them to react more skillfully in real emergencies.

An essential component of efficient emergency planning is personal accountability. Governments and communities have important roles, but people must also take proactive measures to protect their families and themselves. This duty entails keeping up with prospective dangers, participating in emergency exercises, and keeping a personal emergency supply box. In addition to enhancing personal safety, being prepared for emergencies helps emergency response systems function more efficiently, freeing up resources for those who genuinely need them.

The foundation of efficient emergency preparedness and response is communication. During emergencies, having clear routes of communication guarantees that vital information is distributed promptly and adequately. Community-wide communication strategies—such as using social media, emergency alert systems, and traditional media outlets—are essential to keep inhabitants informed. Individual communication plans also improve cooperation and lessen confusion in emergencies by designating specific meeting locations or points of contact.

The effectiveness and efficiency of response operations are increased when technology is included in emergency preparedness. During emergencies, social media platforms, smartphone applications, and emergency alert systems provide real-time information and updates. Using Geographic Information System (GIS) technology, data on vulnerabilities and dangers can be mapped out and analyzed, facilitating more focused and knowledgeable emergency preparation. Additionally, technology makes distant collaboration and communication more accessible, especially when physical access is prohibited.

Hurricanes, earthquakes, and wildfires are natural calamities requiring special attention in emergency planning. Planning and responding to disasters effectively requires an understanding of the distinctive qualities of each kind of calamity. Residents in hurricane-prone locations need to secure their homes, make evacuation plans, and assemble emergency supplies to be ready for strong winds, heavy rain, and storm surges. Safe zones should be established inside homes, bulky furniture should be secured, and emergency supplies should be kept in mind if infrastructure is damaged. Having evacuation plans, establishing defensible spaces surrounding residences, and paying close attention to fire safety precautions are all part of being prepared for wildfires.

Pandemics and disease outbreaks are examples of public health emergencies that call for a different set of preparations. Effective preparedness is facilitated by the timely and correct distribution of information, public education efforts, and the adoption of preventive measures, including immunization programs and cleanliness practices. To handle future spikes in healthcare demand, health systems must also ensure they have enough infrastructure, staff, and medical supplies. Governments, healthcare providers, and the general public must work together to manage public health emergencies effectively.

Specialized emergency preparation is required for industrial accidents, such as chemical spills and nuclear mishaps. Neighboring communities with industrial operations must know about potential dangers, evacuation routes, and safety procedures. To handle chemical or radioactive events, emergency response teams need specialized training, and communication tactics should consider the unique risks involved in these situations. Frequent drills and exercises guarantee that emergency procedures are known to first responders and the general population.

Global crises like the COVID-19 pandemic highlight the significance of worldwide cooperation and readiness in today's interconnected society. Robust public health systems in each nation are necessary for pandemic preparedness, but so is international collaboration in sharing knowledge, resources, and experience. International agencies like the World Health Organization (WHO) are essential for organizing worldwide reactions and ensuring that medical supplies and vaccines are distributed fairly.

Adapting to Changing Circumstances

Life is a journey with many ups and downs, obstacles, and surprising turns. An essential part of the human experience is adjusting to changing conditions, which calls for adaptability, resiliency, and a readiness to accept the unexpected. This section examines the many facets of adaptation and its importance for fostering resilience in the face of uncertainty, managing transitions, and personal growth. The capacity for adaptation becomes evident as we move through the intricate web of life as a fundamental element of development, well-being, and the search for a purposeful and happy life.

Fundamentally, adaptability is a natural trait that characterizes people's ability to adjust to and prosper in various settings. Intellectually, emotionally, and physically, people begin a lifelong path of adaptation when born. As a result of their adaptation to novel sensory stimuli, infants create brain connections that serve as the basis for cognitive development. As people move through different phases of life, adaptation becomes a dynamic process that includes minor tweaks and significant changes.

Adaptability is crucial to personal development, defined by self-discovery and changing identities. Adolescence is a time of increased flexibility, characterized by changes in life's social, emotional, and physical aspects. As a person enters adulthood, they must learn to navigate complex decisions, build connections, and identify their beliefs and goals. A consistent and genuine sense of identity is primarily shaped by one's capacity to adjust to changing self-perceptions and social expectations.

Career paths frequently require negotiating quickly changing professional environments due to sociological, technological, and economic developments. The modern workforce is defined by the requirement for flexibility as new skill sets, job responsibilities, and industry changes occur. People who adopt an attitude of constant learning and flexibility can better deal with the changing demands of the professional world and stay flexible in the face of shifting job markets.

Transitions are important turning points that require adjustment, whether they are forced or decided. Life events that need adjustment to new roles, responsibilities, and emotional landscapes include moving, getting married, becoming a parent, or losing a loved one. Adapting to transitions entails managing internal changes in priorities, views, and values and adjusting to external changes. People who approach changes with adaptability and resiliency frequently come out of them with fresh perspectives and abilities.

Rapid and linked changes, ranging from geopolitical upheavals to technological revolutions, characterize the global scene. Rethinking established norms and systems and exhibiting collective resilience are necessary for society to adjust to these changes. For example, the global emergence of the digital age has changed social interactions, business, and communication. Societies that welcome technological innovation and modify their laws and institutions appropriately set themselves up for success in the changing environment.

Regarding health, the current COVID-19 pandemic is a sobering reminder of the necessity of social and personal adjustment to unanticipated obstacles. The epidemic has forced nations to reevaluate their healthcare systems, put public health measures into place, and expedite the development of vaccines—all of which are examples of adaptive reactions to a fast-changing problem. Individuals have had to modify daily schedules, accept working remotely, and develop creative ways to stay in touch, demonstrating the adaptability and tenacity of humans.

Resilience is strongly related to adaptability; resilience is the capacity to overcome adversity and face problems head-on with a feeling of empowerment. Cultivating coping strategies, encouraging optimism, and creating a support system are all part of building resilience. Resilient people not only adjust to changing conditions well, but they also overcome obstacles with renewed fortitude and insight. It is possible to develop resilience, a dynamic trait, by self-reflection, mindfulness exercises, and the development of social networks.

There are many lessons to be learned about resilience and adaptability from the natural world. Ecosystems are living examples of how species are interconnected and the delicate balance needed for sustainability since they constantly adapt to changing environmental conditions. Biodiversity, a sign of millennia of adaptation, keeps ecosystems resilient to changes in their surroundings. To become resilient to outside threats, human civilizations can learn from nature, which emphasizes the value of diversity, interconnectedness, and sustainable behaviors.

Cultural adaptability reflects cultures' capacity to accept variety, adopt novel concepts, and change throughout time. Cultures resistant to change run the risk of becoming stagnant, whereas adaptive cultures flourish when conditions change. Maintaining traditions and welcoming innovation must coexist dynamically for cultures to adapt culturally and address modern issues simultaneously. This balance must be struck.

Psychological adaptation emphasizes how humans may evolve and find purpose amid hardship, especially when faced with trauma or adversity. According to the positive psychology notion of "post-traumatic growth," people can go through significant personal growth after experiencing trauma. Although the idea does not lessen the suffering or difficulties of trying times, it does emphasize the possibility of resilience and constructive change when people learn to live with and overcome adversity.

CONCLUSION

Through our investigation of "Living Free and Green: A Practical Guide to Off-Grid Independence," we have set a path to a more independent and sustainable way of living. This e-book's chapters have shed light on various off-grid living topics, from learning about sustainable building techniques and eco-friendly energy options to comprehending the factors to be considered when choosing the ideal piece of land. Every chapter has served as a springboard, educating readers on the nuances of off-grid life and equipping them with the knowledge necessary to live more sustainably.

The practical advice provided in this e-book underscores the importance of making informed decisions in all aspects of off-grid living. Whether it's harnessing solar energy, conserving water, or embracing organic practices, the advice offered is designed to foster self-reliance and a deeper connection with nature. As detailed in this guide, off-grid living is more than just a lifestyle choice; it's a philosophy that encapsulates our dedication to reducing our environmental footprint and living harmoniously with the Earth.

As we get to the end of this guide, it is clear that the road to off-grid independence has its challenges. Still, in these difficulties, chances for development and resilience present themselves. A larger ethos that aims to establish a sustainable, regenerative, and interrelated way of life is reflected in the considerations for waste reduction, water management, and sustainable construction, which go beyond simple advice.

This e-book has proven to be an invaluable resource, shedding light on numerous facets of off-grid living. It serves as a rallying cry for those seeking to cultivate environmental consciousness, personal liberty, and a more sustainable future. By equipping individuals with the knowledge required to make choices that favor off-grid living, this website empowers them to become guardians of the environment and architects of their own freedom.

With a vision of a future where living freely and sustainably is not just a dream but a collective reality, readers are equipped with practical knowledge and inspired as they explore the realms of renewable energy, sustainable building materials, and self-reliant practices. This book guides readers towards a lifestyle that celebrates the beauty of resilience, simplicity, and a deep bond with nature. The path to off-grid independence is a transformative one. Let this book ignite positive change in the spirit of off-grid and eco- friendly living, inspiring individuals to embrace off-grid life to create a more sustainable and peaceful world.